Serving Teens with Mental Illness in the Library

SERVING TEENS WITH MENTAL ILLNESS IN THE LIBRARY

A Practical Guide

Deborah K. Takahashi

Libraries Unlimited Professional Guides for
Young Adult Librarians Series
C. Allen Nichols and Mary Anne Nichols, Series Editors

An Imprint of ABC-CLIO, LLC
Santa Barbara, California • Denver, Colorado

Library of Congress Cataloging-in-Publication Data

Names: Takahashi, Deborah K., author.
Title: Serving teens with mental illness in the library : a practical guide / Deborah K. Takahashi.
Description: Santa Barbara : ABC-CLIO, [2019] | Series: Libraries unlimited professional guides for young adult librarians | Includes bibliographical references and index. |
Identifiers: LCCN 2019008328 (print) | LCCN 2019010928 (ebook) | ISBN 9781440862779 (ebook) | ISBN 9781440862762 (pbk. : alk. paper)
Subjects: LCSH: Libraries and the mentally ill. | Libraries and teenagers.
Classification: LCC Z711.92.M42 (ebook) | LCC Z711.92.M42 T35 2019 (print) | DDC 027.6/63—dc23
LC record available at https://lccn.loc.gov/2019008328

ISBN: 978-1-4408-6276-2 (paperback)
        978-1-4408-6277-9 (ebook)

23 22 21 20 19   1 2 3 4 5

This book is also available as an eBook.

Libraries Unlimited
An Imprint of ABC-CLIO, LLC

ABC-CLIO, LLC
147 Castilian Drive
Santa Barbara, California 93117
www.abc-clio.com

This book is printed on acid-free paper ∞

Manufactured in the United States of America

To All the Teens I Have Met

Thank you for teaching me how to advocate for you and for telling me to never give up. You have shown me how to keep on fighting for teens who need help and demonstrating how brave all of you really are.

To All the Teen Librarians I Know

Without your passion, the impact you have on your teens and your community would not be as bright without your shining light.

CONTENTS

SERIES FOREWORD

As the number of mental health–related diagnoses of all people but especially of teens rises, those working with teens need to know how to recognize common symptoms and what resources to recommend. Thankfully, more people are talking honestly about mental health since it lessens the stigma associated with it. Determining how to help teens whose symptoms may look like common adolescent behavior can be a challenge. We are grateful that Deborah Takahashi can educate us on navigating these challenges. She draws upon her experience as a librarian as well as someone who has earned a Youth Mental Health First Aid certification to provide those working with and advocating for teens' guidance, seasoned advice, and a plan for service.

We are proud of our association with Libraries Unlimited/ABC-CLIO, which continues to prove itself as the premier publisher of books to help library staff serve teens. This series has succeeded because our authors know the needs of those library employees who work with young adults. Without exception, they have written useful and practical handbooks for library staff. Deborah's practical advice will inspire you to provide an environment for teens where they are comfortable asking for and receiving information vital to maintaining their mental health.

We hope you find this book, as well as our entire series, to be informative, providing you with valuable ideas as you serve teens and that this work will further inspire you to do great things to make teens welcome in your library. If you have an idea for a title that could be added to our series or would like to submit a book proposal, please e-mail us at bittner@abc-clio.com. We'd love to hear from you!

Mary Anne Nichols
C. Allen Nichols

PREFACE

When I decided to become a librarian in 2006, I had no idea that I would become a teen mental health advocate. In 2008, after recovering from my one and, hopefully, only major depressive disorder, I got my first full-time position as a teen library assistant. Over the next six years, I came to know many amazing young people who have had a profound effect on my life. This fueled my passion to advocate for teens, and I have since dedicated my career to making sure that teens are prepared to tackle anything but, at the same time, know they are supported and cared for.

As someone who experienced depression, I know that mental illness is nothing to be ashamed of. In fact, mental illness is just like any other illness that can be managed. Furthermore, people with mental illness can and do live very successful lives. It is important that teens be made aware of this. While teens come into the library for all sorts of reasons, there will always be a handful of teens who see the library as the only place they feel safe enough to ask for help. If you find yourself in a situation with one of these teens, know that you can help, even if only by listening. This may sound uncomfortable, but rest assured that you are not expected to diagnose or provide medical care. Unless you are a licensed clinical social worker, psychologist, or a psychiatrist, you are not obligated to treat teens with mental illness and, in fact, should not attempt to do so. However, as a teen advocate, you should know that you have what it takes to help the teens in need, which is why I wrote this book.

Teen librarians do amazing things every day for teens, and this includes ensuring teens have access to programs and information that will help them develop the skills and the aptitude to succeed in life. By addressing mental illness in the library, you can provide that beacon of hope for teens who might be scared or know someone who is struggling with mental illness. Teen librarianship is no longer just about books—it is about getting to know the teen community and making your library presence known and vital to the community. Within these pages, you will find resources to help you prepare and support teens with mental illness. In addition, you will find advice that will encourage you to provide teens with the information they need to get help for themselves, their friends, and/or their family.

By picking up this book, you have demonstrated your courage and willingness to learn more about mental illness and how you can play a crucial part in supporting the well-being of your teen patrons. I hope this book provides you with what you need to get started, and I am excited to see what all of you will come up with to bring mental illness to center stage.

—*Deborah K. Takahashi*

ACKNOWLEDGMENTS

This book could not have been done without the encouragement from my colleague Jane Gov. Your vision, passion, and talent encouraged me to write this book, and your support really pushed me to finish so thank you from the bottom of my heart. I also want to thank the Pasadena Public Library Teen Advisory Board for your creativity and your desire to serve those in need. Teens, like you, make this world a better place, and I hope this book can help pave the way to that future. Thank-you to all the teens who allowed me to watch them grow from teens to adults (Amberly, Dennis, Carmen, and Koni). Thank-you to Eric and Coleman for giving me the drive and the fortitude to finish this book so thanks for letting me into your lives and helping me become the librarian and youth advocate I am today.

A huge thank-you to my dearest friends Crystal and Tara. Every time I wanted to give up, you both said, "You can do it!" To my colleagues Tanya, Asbed, and Ann Marie, for cheering me on through this process and for lending an ear when I got frustrated. I also want to thank my editors, Barbara Ittner and Mary Anne Nichols, for guiding me through this process and for your feedback. Your guidance and advice helped me become a better writer, and I will always be grateful for that.

Last, but not least, I want to thank my husband, William, for being so patient and supportive during this whole process. There were many nights of writing that took over the dining room table, but you always supplied me with a caffeinated beverage and kept the kitties busy as I typed away. Thank you for always telling me that I needed to do this.

INTRODUCTION

In 2015, the Centers for Disease Control and Prevention (CDC) released a study[1] that documented the rise of teen suicide between 1975 and 2015. In 1975, 1,289 males and 305 females aged 15–19 years died by suicide. In 2015, the number of deaths by suicide in the same age group increased to 1,537 males and 524 females. In the last 43 years, the number of suicides increased by 31 percent among males, whereas death by suicide among teens girls increased by 5 percent. Given these staggering statistics, suicide has now become one of the major leading causes of death among teens. Why? Studies have shown that bullying, violence, and mental illness are some of the causes.

Teen librarians and staff are tackling more complex and complicated issues that the world has ever seen before. Given the rise in poverty and unemployment and the increase in violence and hostility against marginalized groups of teens, teen librarians and library staff are now faced with a new challenge that changes what it means to be a librarian. According to "The Future of Library Services for and with Teens: A Call to Action,"[2] published by the Young Adult Library Services Association (YALSA), libraries are being called to help teens reach their potential by preparing them for future. Furthermore, libraries are taking a stand to fight the injustices that are affecting teens today. In other words, librarians are not just advocates for literacy but advocates for teens.

The purpose of *Serving Teens with Mental Illness in the Library: A Practical Guide* is to encourage teen librarians and staff to participate in today's mental health movement, which is to destigmatize mental illness through advocacy, provide teens with access to mental health resources to manage their mental illness, and explain how to model and demonstrate advocacy to teens. While this book encourages teen librarians and staff to learn more about mental illness, and how to assist teens in crisis, it does not ask, or require, readers to diagnose and treat teens with mental illness. As information specialists, you have the skills to guide teens to resources but are not, whatsoever, obligated to become a teen's case worker, nor should you be.

This book provides readers with information about teen brain development and how mental illness can affect a teen's ability to function and thrive in today's world. Moreover, readers will learn about resources that can help them prepare for teens' mental health crisis and techniques to assist them in the event of an emergency. Instructions on how to build a teen mental health initiative that addresses the need for teen mental health information and education are also included, along with strategies for how to partner with local mental health organizations to bring services into the library and promote a dialogue with the teen population. Through your efforts, you have the chance to invite the teen community to participate in the creation of an initiative that not only empowers teens but provides them with opportunity to demonstrate empathy and compassion for those who are unable to speak up for themselves.

In addition, you'll find practical insight on how to track your progress, evaluate outcomes, and create a master plan to actively engage your new partners to continue growing the teen mental health initiative. Lastly, there is a section that provides basic tips and techniques for creating a self-care plan and why it's important that you care for yourself when interacting with teens experiencing mental illness. Hopefully, by reading this book and learning about teens with mental illness, you'll be in a better position to serve not just teens who are experiencing mental illness but all members of your community.

NOTES

1. "*QuickStats:* Suicide Rates for Teens Aged 15–19 Years, by Sex—United States, 1975–2015." Morbidity and Mortality Weekly Report (MMWR). 2017, 66: 816. http://dx.doi.org/10.15585/mmwr.mm6630a6.
2. "The Future of Library Services for and with Teens: Project Report," American Library Association. September 17, 2013. http://www.ala.org/yaforum/future-library-services-and-teens-project-report.

1

◇ ◇ ◇

THE TEEN BRAIN AND
MENTAL ILLNESS

Before taking a deep dive into the topic of teen mental illness, you need to understand the basics of adolescence. "Adolescence" is typically defined as the years between childhood and adulthood, which roughly translates between 12 and 18 years old. However, adolescence is more than just a milestone—it often happens to be the most difficult time in a young person's life. As teens start to navigate their world, what they, and their parents, don't realize is that their brains and bodies are developing at very different stages. Due to this dysrhythmia, teens are often confused and disoriented, which not only is frustrating but can even be terrifying at times. As teens enter adolescence, you, as adult advocates, will likely notice behaviors that make it difficult to differentiate between typical adolescent behavior and mental illness. Although librarians are not trained experts when it comes to neurology and psychology, nor should you be, understanding how the teen brain works at this point in time can be of tremendous help. By observing and recognizing why teens do what they do, you can determine if something else might be going wrong. With this knowledge, not only can you prepare for difficult conversations but you can help teens advocate for their health and well-being.

When observing, or even thinking about teenagers, you don't see them as children, but you don't see them as adults either. What is impossible to see is the biological race that teens are undergoing. In other words, there is a lot going on in the body of a young person who is trying to get by the best that he or she can. No one is born with the innate ability to predict what's going to happen in the future, and, for teens, they are not only dealing with the guessing game called life, but their bodies are undergoing a series of physical and hormonal changes that can cause extra complications in their lives. On the one hand, teens have a better understanding of abstract concepts such as privilege and morality. Also, teens are developing their identities and are more assertive in how they want to be perceived and treated. However, along with these mature thoughts and feelings, teens are still developing, physically: their bodies are changing and are experiencing discomfort as well as new sexual desires. As puberty does what it's supposed to, the teen brain is also developing. By understanding adolescent development, you will have a better understanding of why teens behave the way they do and what to expect during these turbulent years.

ADOLESCENT DEVELOPMENT IN A NUTSHELL

Take a moment and reflect on your adolescence. Remember the good things, but also think about the bad things. What about your adolescence has helped you develop into the adult that you are today? For some of you, it may be kind of amazing that you survived at all. For others, it may be a time you want to forget. It's important to look at adolescence not just from a personal point of view but also from a scientific and biological point of view. Granted, the term "adults" is subjective (some teens can be more mature and smarter than some adults); what separates a 16-year-old version of us from the 35-year-old is that the 35-year-old brain is fully developed. Even though teens can be smarter and quicker than adults, it doesn't mean they have the "know-how" on the skills it takes to become an adult. In other words, teens may look and talk like adults, but, in reality, they haven't the slightest idea what it means to be an "adult."

Adolescence is not just about the actual brain; it's about the physical, emotional, and cognitive development as well. Teens start to feel and understand complex emotions such as lust, love, disappointment, and loss. Unfortunately, for many adults, especially those who don't work or know how teens are, the most popular words that are synonymous with teens are negative: "moody," "selfish," "emotional," "angst," and so on. Although some of these terms are on point when it comes to adolescents, it's important to keep in mind that there is a biological explanation as to why teens have a hard time dealing with difficult situations. For example, when it comes to handling rejections, teens may become very upset or angry, which is why they seem temperamental. Another example is when they are being antagonized by their parents or other adults, which is why they will either ignore or lash out at them.

As the body continues to develop, so does the brain. Teens are start-ing to realize that in order to be a part of the "adult" world, they need to figure out their purpose and how they are going to get there. Rather than depending on their parents, teens seek out activities, peers, and other adults who can help them find that purpose and somehow, some way, help them function in the adult world. These components in a teen's world are huge milestones in adolescence, which is why it's important to understand biology and typical adolescent behavior versus behaviors that are indicative of mental illness.

ADOLESCENT BEHAVIOR

So what exactly is typical adolescent development? The World Health Organization (WHO) defines adolescence as "a period of life with specific health and developmental needs and rights. It is also a time to develop knowledge and skills, learn to manage emotions and relationships, and acquire attributes and abilities that will be important for enjoying the ado-lescent years and assuming adults."[1] In addition, the WHO outlines other important key points[2] such as the following:

- Adolescence is one of the most rapid phases of human develop-ment.
- Biological maturity precedes psychosocial maturity. This has implications for policy and program responses to the exploration and experimentation that takes place during adolescence.
- The characteristics of both the individual and the environment influence the changes taking place during adolescence.
- Younger adolescents may be particularly vulnerable when their capacities are still developing and they are beginning to move outside the confines of their families.
- The changes in adolescence have health consequences not only in adolescence but also over their life course.
- The unique nature and importance of adolescence mandates explicit and specific attention in health policy and programs.

While development influences a teen's behavior, there are a few things worth noting. During this period, there are several things occurring at once: physical development and cognitive development. During puberty, the most notable physical changes take on the form of increased body hair, growth spurts, and the development of the sex organs. As this transformation occurs, the brain is undergoing its own evolution, which isn't as rapid as the physical changes and often causes trouble for most teens. Since teens are very much aware that their bodies are changing, their behavior reflects how they are feeling, which explains why some teens are very self-conscious about their bodies and are reluctant to share how they are feeling. In order to understand teen behavior, it's important to know more about the source of these processes, starting with the brain.

The Adolescent Brain

The human brain functions as the epicenter of what makes you who you are. Although the human brain doesn't look like much other than an ugly, wrinkly mass of tissue, it contains millions of structures that fit within every crevice, each of which has specific purposes and missions. To better understand the living and functioning brain, try googling a brain MRI and notice that this organ is made up of two types of matter (gray matter and white matter) and two hemispheres made up of four different lobes. These lobes are responsible for a lot of things. Within them are brain cells called neurons that are connected to nerve fibers (synapses), which communicate and send signals all through the brain to keep the person alive and functional. As children, the synapses exist to absorb information, and, the more you learn, the more you grow synapses. However, as you get older, the brain has this built-in mechanism to cut off or "prune" most of these synapses as the brain has learned to do what it needs without the help of the synapses. Along with this pruning, the gray matter, which houses millions of the neurons and is the thickest layer of the cerebral cortex, undergoes construction to become more efficient and much faster. This is what happens as puberty occurs and why teens are able to multitask so well.

As for white matter, which is made up of nerve fibers called axons, it is responsible for speeding up the nerve signals between the different lobes. These lobes house a variety of functions that are not only responsible for unconscious activities such as breathing and blinking but are responsible for personality traits, muscle memory, comprehension, and many other things. What's even more fascinating is that these lobes are connected through a series of wires to your senses, which means when you are hungry and want ice cream, your sight tells the brain, "Eat ice cream," and your taste signals to your brain to say, "Yum."

Now that you know a little more about the structure that makes up the brain, let's learn more about the lobes and what they are responsible for.

Frontal lobe

- Movement
  - Ability to move your arms when you swim or hug someone
- Motivation
  - Wanting to hug a puppy because it's cute
- Socialization
  - Ability to interact with friends and even strangers
- Self-expression
  - Using language that is deliberate
- Forms the short-term memory
  - Ability to remember passwords to your social media logins and knowing how to log in each time

Parietal lobe:

- Sensory processing
  - Recognizing textures, colors, smells, and taste
- Create visual spatial relationships
  - Ability to see a chair and sit down without falling
- Writing and arithmetic
  - Ability to calculate in your minds and writing out what you want to say
- Knowing your space
  - Being aware of where you are in space

Temporal lobe:

- Auditory processing
  - Processing sounds, language, words, and music
- Other sensory functions
- Assisting in other parts of the limbic system such as smell
- Forms the long-term memory
  - Ability to remember your earliest memories and complete repetitive tasks such as brushing teeth, washing face, and combing hair

Occipital lobe:

- Home to the visual cortex
  - Ability to process anything sight-related

By the time children have entered adolescence, they have managed to accomplish quite a bit in their young lives. In fact, they have developed about 80 percent of their brain. However, teens still have a very long way to go because the parts that are responsible for rational decision making and other adultlike traits have yet to develop. According to Dr. Frances E. Jensen (2015), author of the insightful book *The Teenage Brain: A Neuroscientist's Survival Guide to Raising Adolescents and Young Adults*, "The teenage brain is like a brand-new Ferrari: it's primed and pumped, but it hasn't been road tested yet. In other words, it's all revved up but doesn't quite know here to go."[3] To learn more about the teenage brain, here is another great book to help you dive deeper into the teen brain:

Siegel, Daniel J. *Brainstorm: The Power and Purpose of the Teenage Brain.* New York: Penguin Group USA, 2015.

Notably, during the development process, some parts of the brain are working better than the others. In fact, the brain develops from the back to the front where connectivity between the frontal (the part of the brain that is responsible for behavior, personality, and learning) and the occipital lobe (which is often referred to as the visual cortex) takes a long time to develop. Since teen brains have reached 80 percent of their maturity, the other 20 percent explains why teens often do things that just don't make sense to adults. For example, if you ask a teen, "Why did you think it was a good idea to use the Emergency Exit and set off the alarm?" he or she would reply, "I don't know . . . my friends dared me." There is a reason why teens do silly things and it's because they are literally missing 20 percent of their brain. Obviously, this rationale is only part of a bigger problem as to why teens don't always make the best decisions, but, when it comes to tolerating these behaviors in your library, you need to understand what's going on in the minds of teens, which, unfortunately, not a lot of us learned in library school.

As a teen librarian, you probably have a high tolerance when it comes to goofy teen behavior, but, at the same time, you have to know when enough is enough. Deep down, we all love being one of the "cool" adults in the lives of our teens, but it's also important to demonstrate your authority when needed. Specifically, as you welcome teens to stay and chill in your building, be sure to explain the rules and regulations and explain that teens will be held accountable for their behaviors, which leads to another aspect of adolescence that can be very frustrating, that is, a teen's need for autonomy.

Teens and Autonomy

As teens actively look for ways to gain independence, the first thing they are going to do is distance themselves from their parents. By pulling themselves away from their parents, teens begin to rely more heavily on their peers and social networks to gather the information they need to find their place in the world. At the same time, teens may equate other adults with their parents, which accounts not only for bad behavior toward their elders but for their reluctance to confide in someone they see as the equivalent of their parents. As a teen librarian, you may have seen what this autonomy looks like but have come to respect it. If you have worked with teens before, you know that you usually get a mixed bag of teens who use the library. There are the teens who want absolutely nothing to do with any adult, teens who want us to be their next best friend, and teens who are cordial but have no interest in chatting as they have mountains of homework to do. However, there are those teens who genuinely want to be there in the library and get to know us but are shy or totally inexperienced with approaching adults.

> About eight years ago, there was one teen whom I would greet every day and he would see me, but quickly put his head down and take a seat. Eventually, this teen would become a teen advisory board member, and, I continued to mentor him as he was almost done with college. Although it took me at least four different occasions to get him to loosen up, I am happy I pestered him to say "hello" because he is an extraordinary young man. So what did I learn from this experience? I learned to not take it personally if a teen does not want to talk but treat it as a lesson in patience and persistence. Is there the possibility that it took a while for him to trust me because he was scared of me or trying to assert his autonomy?

Teens resist adults for a variety of reasons, including:

a) Cultural reasons (i.e., some cultures view mental illness as a sign of weakness or it's taboo to talk about such things).
b) The teen is inexperienced with adults and does not know what to do, or say, around an adult who is not his or her parent.
c) The teen doesn't have good relationships with other adults in his or her life.

Whatever the reasons for teen aloofness, you are an adult who exists to help them whether they ask for it or not. Furthermore, you need to make it known to these teens that they matter and if they need help with anything they can rely on you.

Along with their need for autonomy, teens are starting to experiment within their own social circles and social behaviors, which isn't a bad thing. Whether it's forming a coven of fellow goths, joining a sports team, or hanging out with fellow musicians, these social circles are important for teens to maintain. The main drawback to these alliances is when teens start to experiment and engage in riskier and, sometimes, dangerous behaviors (i.e., substance use thrill seeking, and having unprotected sex). According to White and Swartzwelder (2013, p. 21), "Risk taking comes from the desire to explore the world and to find out how things work. The fact that the urge to take chances is strong in adolescence, when the brain is elastic and primed for learning, explains why this time of exploration and experimentation is an opportunity for neurological and psychological growth—as well as a dangerous period for teens who don't know when to say when."[4] These risky behaviors can often be attributed to the underdeveloped frontal lobe. Teens want to be liked and accepted for who they are, but there will be times when teens do not make the best decisions. Despite the consequences of these decisions, what's even more worrisome is if those behaviors are accepted, or respected, by their peers, teens may come to rely on these behaviors that could have a significant impact on their mental health. As teens seek their place in this world, not only are they grappling with major physical and cognitive changes but their emotions are literally pulling them in every direction. While this is bound to happen in the lives of teens, there is a fine line between being emotional and the onset of mental illness.

TEEN PSYCHOLOGICAL DEVELOPMENT

While the brain develops, there are other processes occurring as well. Joe Lewis (1991) discusses Kohlberg's levels and six stages of moral development, which differ from Piaget and Erickson's theories in that these stages did not rely on age. The levels and stages are listed below. Additional information for each of these can be found in Lewis (1991).

Level One: Preconventional Morality
    Stage One: Punishment and obedience orientation
    Stage Two: Instrumental relativist orientation
Level Two: Conventional morality
    Stage Three: Interpersonal concordance or "good boy/nice girl orientation"
    Stage Four: "Law and order" orientation

Level Three: Postconventional morality
   Stage Five: Social contract, legalistic orientation
   Stage Six: Universal ethical principle orientation

All of these behaviors are indicative of the changes that are occurring in the part of the brain known as the amygdala, which is responsible for processing emotions and just happens to be the de facto part of the brain that teens rely on since their frontal lobe hasn't fully developed. What's most astounding about adolescent psychological development is how aware teens are of the changes that are happening in their bodies. Given this awareness, teens' behavior is greatly affected by these changes, which is why it's important to pay attention to their behavior.

TYPICAL TEEN BEHAVIOR VERSUS MENTAL ILLNESS

Adolescence is a turbulent time in young people's lives because their body is doing one thing while their mind is doing another. This can have a profound effect on how they respond to certain situations and if they will seek help. Take a look at the following scenarios:

Scenario 1:

Librarian: Hi Erin! What's up!
Erin: I totally embarrassed myself in front of Chris and I want to die!
Librarian: What do you mean?
Erin: I meant to tell him "Hello!" and I totally froze! Can't believe I did that!

Scenario 2:

Librarian: Hi, David. How are you?
David: Not good. I hate my life and I want it all to end. In fact, I am going to end it today.

Scenario 3:

Librarian: Hey Luna!
Luna: Hello.
Librarian: Everything okay? You've been kinda down lately. In fact, it's been a while since I have seen you smile.
Luna: Oh. Everything is okay. Just tired and life has been a little crazy. I'll be fine.

In scenario 1, Erin is just being melodramatic because she embarrassed herself in front of a boy she likes. However, in scenario 2, David expressed he wants to end his life immediately, which conveys David may be suicidal. In scenario 3, Luna's behavior has changed and it seems like she might be depressed. Perhaps you may never come across a teen like David, and you might ask yourself, "Why would a teen feel so hopeless that he or she would want to die?" Although there is no easy answer to this question, these are just a few examples that draw the line between the typical adolescent behavior and teens experiencing mental illness. While teens are already a whirlwind of emotions, the kind of behaviors that David and Luna are experiencing is not a normal adolescent behavior. In most cases, mental illness during adolescence either stems from experiences that have negatively impacted the teen or from genetic factors (i.e., there may be family history of mental illness). What you really need to think about is not why David wanted to die by suicide, but what were the signs he was exhibiting prior to his threat and why didn't anyone see or say anything? What you really need to think about is what to do about it.

For teens who are experiencing mental illness, you need to know the warning signs. One classic sign is moodiness. Moodiness is probably one of the most confounding aspects of adolescence that makes it difficult to tell if a teen is feeling "blue" or if he or she is struggling with life. So how do you know if a teen is just being "moody" or if he or she is suffering from a mental illness? Moodiness is an interchangeable emotion where a teen can be super happy one moment and angry the next. Moodiness is part of normal adolescent development and, most of the time, resolves itself as the teen moves on quickly. However, if this moodiness lasts for more than a few weeks and the teen's behaviors shift from sad to agitated, this would be indicative of mental illness.

When teens start experiencing dramatic shifts in moods, they may also experience other signs that could have an impact on their ability to interact with others and complete daily tasks such as going to school. In fact, one in five[5] teens will develop a serious mental health disorder that can affect his or her daily life, which is why it's important that parents, mentors, and, yes, teen librarians know the signs.

Signs of Mental Illness

- Withdrawal from social circles and/or activities
- Change in physical appearance (e.g., looking disheveled or extremely tired, substantial weight loss or gain, lack of cleanliness)

- Engagement in risky behavior (drugs and alcohol use, frequent or promiscuous sexual activity)
- Low or agitated moods, extreme mood swings
- Signs of increased anger and hostility (e.g., violent or obscene language, physical violence)
- Indications of extreme duress (constant fidgeting, shortness of breath, paranoid behavior)
- Loss of interest in favorite activities, general disinterest in life
- Visible injuries due to self-harm (e.g., cuts or bruises)
- Expressions of suicidal thoughts

If a teen's behaviors reflect any of these signs, and they have lasted for more than two weeks, it is important that you talk to the teen to see what's going on. If the teen is willing to talk about what's been happening to him or her, be sure to listen without judgment. If the teen asks for help, it's your responsibility to guide him or her to appropriate resources, just like it's your responsibility to help adults and children find information they are looking for. Again, you are not a trained medical professional, but you are an information specialist who can find the right kind of information to provide for teens in crisis.

Mental illness can be treated and managed. What's troublesome is that of the one in five teens who are diagnosed with mental illness, only half will seek out treatment. The longer a teen goes without treatment, the higher the chance that the teen will have even more problems as an adult. Mental illness makes its debut during the teen years, but it does not fully manifest until the young adult years, which is why it's important that teens get the help they need right away and not wait for 10 years from now.

It's important to let teens know that if they have a mental illness, there is absolutely nothing wrong with them. There are hundreds of thousands of people who live with mental illness and lead completely normal lives. If teens feel embarrassed or ashamed, let them know that what they are going through can be resolved with the right treatment so it's crucial to do your best to reassure them that they will be okay. These situations are never easy, but, as a teen librarian, it's part of your job to advocate for those who don't know how to advocate for themselves.

NOTES

1. "Adolescent Development." World Health Organization. May 9, 2017. http://www.who.int/maternal_child_adolescent/topics/adolescence/development/en/.

2. Ibid.
3. Jensen, Frances E. *The Teenage Brain: A Neuroscientist's Survival Guide to Raising Adolescents and Young Adults*. New York: Harper Paperbacks, 2016. 26–27.
4. White, Aaron M., and Scott Swartzwelder. *What Are They Thinking?!: The Straight Facts about the Risk-Taking, Social-Networking, Still-Developing Teen Brain*. New York: W.W. Norton & Company, 2013. 21; Lewis, Joe. "91.05.07: The Physiological and Psychological Development of the Adolescent." May 7, 1991. http://teachersinstitute.yale.edu/curriculum/units/1991/5/91.05.07.x.html.
5. "Mental Disorders." Teen Mental Health. 2018. http://teenmentalhealth.org/learn/mental-disorders/.

2

◇ ◇ ◇

THE MANY FACES OF
MENTAL ILLNESS

The American Psychiatric Association (APA) defines mental health as "effective functioning in daily activities resulting in a person's ability to be productive, sustain healthy relationships, and be able to cope and overcome adversity."[1] If a person is unable to stay productive, to maintain healthy relationships, or is fearful of leaving his or her home, it means the person might be experiencing a mental disorder. These may be signs of mental illness. Although scientists and medical professionals have concluded that mental health challenges are legitimate health problems, like diabetes or high blood pressure, mental illness is a result of certain brain-based disorders known as mental disorders.

In the fifth edition of the *Diagnostic Statistical Manual of Mental Disorders* (*DSM-5*), there are over 200 classified mental disorders. These disorders have been grouped by specific characteristics that people may experience such as mood, behavior, and their being prone to psychosis. Given the strides that have been made in diagnosing mental disorders, there have been multiple studies to confirm that some mental disorders may result from genetics.[2] Although there is no blood test for these disorders, there is now evidence that can be found in DNA. When someone is diagnosed with a mental disorder, one of the questions a doctor may ask is if there is a family history to see if the person is predisposed to a particular mental disorder. As there are no tests or scans that can detect, or even prevent, a mental disorder, there are certain things you can learn to help guide teens to resources that can get them the help they need.

What sets adults apart from teens are that adults are more aware of their well-being as their brains have fully matured. As noted in the previous chapter, teen bodies and minds are not totally in sync with each other. In fact, teens don't realize these changes as they don't have the breadth of experience to judge themselves objectively, which is why it's so difficult to differentiate between typical and atypical adolescent behavior. However, there are often obvious signs that may indicate that something might be wrong. While teens are a lot tougher than most usually give them credit for, their level of resiliency is impeccable, which is why it's so easy to say that teens bounce back quickly, but, when a teen is unable to "snap" out of a destructive behavior or thought pattern, then there is cause for concern.

Before assuming a teen is experiencing a mental disorder, observe his or her behavior. Is the teen stressed out because of an infinite amount of homework? Is the teen struggling to juggle his or her school work and part-time job to help put food on the table? Stress has a huge impact on a teen's ability to cope with daily life, so if a teen seems overwhelmed it might be worthwhile to sit down and talk to him or her. Another factor that can impact a teen's mental health is his or her home and/or school environment. Environment plays a big role in a teen's life because this is where direct influences come from. Whether they are wealthy or live in poverty, what happens at home affects teens. If a teen confides in you that life at home is not so great, keep in mind that teens who are exposed to neglect and/or abuse are more likely to develop a mental disorder. If you know that a teen is struggling at home, you can guide the teen to resources that could save his or her life or at least remove, or protect, the teen from that toxic environment by developing coping mechanisms and self-care routines.

Although genetics, stress, and environment are three common factors that negatively impact teen mental health, there are other factors such as trauma, bullying, and peer pressure that can also lead to mental illness, and they don't necessarily stem from biology and environment. In fact, teens are grappling with so many issues all at once that it's no wonder they are being diagnosed with anxiety and depression at an early age. As a teen librarian, and youth advocate, you have a unique opportunity to help teens cope in this world without having MD attached to your title. Given the signs of normal adolescent development and mental illness, what follows is a list of mental health challenges that can begin in early adolescence and develop over a period of time.

ANXIETY DISORDERS

According to the National Institute of Mental Health (NIMH) "anxiety is prolonged instances of anxiousness that has a significant impact on daily living."[3] It's okay to feel anxious every now and then, but people who develop anxiety disorders don't ever feel like their anxiety will go away and, unfortunately, can get worse over time without treatment. There are several different types of anxiety disorders, but the most prevalent include general anxiety disorder, panic disorder, post-traumatic stress disorder, and obsessive-compulsive disorder.

Generalized Anxiety Disorder (GAD)

Generalized anxiety disorder, or GAD, is a disorder where people exhibit signs of excessive worry. Whether it's getting ready to take a test, trying to get a job, or applying for college, young people who experience GAD will experience intense feelings of fear and worry to the point they are unable to calm themselves down.

Signs of Generalized Anxiety Disorder

- Excessive worrying and unrealistic fear
- Unable to handle to uncertainty
- Inability to relax
- Difficulty concentrating
- Mood swings (irritability, anger, nervousness)
- Heart palpitations
- Short and shallow breathing
- Dizziness and/or sweating
- Body aches and pains
- Difficulty sleeping

With GAD, it's a slow, growing disorder, where a few anxious thoughts can grow into more within a period of six months. If a teen is experiencing these signs, it's important to know how long he or she has been having these anxious thoughts. It's always good to know the signs of GAD to see if the teen needs professional help. If left untreated, teens with GAD can develop other mental health disorders, such as depression, and may even attempt suicide.

There are several types of treatment that teens can receive, which include medication, psychotherapy, or a combination of both. Teens should be encouraged to follow their treatment plans to manage their signs. While librarians are not medical professionals and are unable to give diagnosis, you can definitely educate yourself as to what can be done and establish connections with organizations that might be able to help teens experiencing anxiety disorders.

Panic Disorder

Panic disorder is another type of anxiety disorder that involves a reoccurring series of sudden panic attacks. Just like anxiousness, some of us have experienced a panic attack, which is usually triggered by a traumatic event.

Signs of Panic Disorder

- Sudden and often-repeated attacks of intense fear
- Feeling out of control during a panic attack
- Extreme avoidance of places and situations that may result in a panic attack
- Rapid heartbeat, shallow breathing, and dizziness
- Weakness, body aches and pains, and sweating

About three years ago, I accidently closed my front door on my kitten's paw. He made this horrible noise and I thought I had broken his paw. I could literally hear my heart pounding in my ears, and I felt like I was going to pass out because I was so scared. Although the kitten was okay in the end (after an hour wait in the pet emergency room and $130 shot of Tylenol), I was traumatized, and I will never, ever forget how scared I was. For those of you who have experienced moments of absolute terror and worry, imagine experiencing that terror several times a week with no warning. Teens who experience panic attacks on a frequent basis eventually develop panic disorder.

There is a visible set of signs that teens may exhibit during a panic attack, and it's good to get familiar with panic disorder symptoms as you may need to step in and help teens gain their bearings. Again, teens can seek out professional help to manage their signs with either medication or cognitive behavior therapy, which teaches teens how to change their negative thoughts and behaviors into more positive and productive thoughts and behaviors. You can definitely support teens with panic disorder by providing them with a quiet space to calm down and a friendly face to talk to, if need be.

Post-Traumatic Stress Disorder (PTSD)

Post-Traumatic Stress Disorder, or PTSD, often occurs after a traumatic event, such as war, an accident, sexual assault, or surviving a natural disaster such as an earthquake, tornado, hurricane, or fire. However, these are not the only events that can cause PTSD, as the death of a loved one can also induce PTSD. PTSD refers to the way a person responds to a frightening event. Normally, when a distressing event occurs, humans go into the "fight or flight" mode, where their bodies and minds automatically respond to the situation. When this happens, it's typical to develop signs of distress, also known as acute stress disorder. While these signs will eventually subside in time, teens who develop PTSD are unable to engage this mode, which is why they may freeze up, black out, or react violently to certain events. If you know that a teen has been struggling after experiencing a terrifying event, it's important to recognize the signs of PTSD, which have been categorized as the re-experiencing the trauma, avoidance, hyperarousal, and mood signs such as the following:

Signs of Post-Traumatic Stress Disorder

Re-experiencing the Trauma

- Experiencing reoccurring dreams, or thoughts, that might relate to the trauma they have experienced
- Experiencing flashbacks, nightmares, or have terrifying thoughts that can induce physical symptoms such as sweating, rapid heartbeat, dizziness, and/or shallow breath

Avoidance

- Avoiding situations that may trigger their anxiety (i.e., if a teen is involved in an auto accident, he or she will avoid riding in cars)
- Blocking out the trauma, where a teen cannot remember what happened to him or her in the first place

Hyperarousal

- Overexcited to the point a teen is unable to concentrate, eat, and sleep
- Exhibiting signs such as aggressiveness or being easily startled
- Hyperarousal symptoms are usually constant and not triggered

Mood Symptoms

- Teens can experience all kinds of mood symptoms with PTSD, which range from feeling guilty to not feeling at all
- The intensity of fear can exacerbate a teen's anxiety

PTSD is classified as an anxiety disorder, but, without intervention or treatment, this disorder can manifest into other disorders, such as depression, bipolar depression, other anxiety disorders and substance use disorders as he or she may self-medicate with alcohol and/or drugs. Fortunately, there are treatment options that teens can investigate, which include a combination of medication (antidepressants, antipsychotics, and mood stabilizers), psychotherapy (talking things out one on one or in a group), and substance rehabilitation. PTSD is treatable when teens can manage their signs successfully, but if left untreated, the teens may suffer long-term effects, such as developing other mental illness, living in extreme fear, and losing relationships.

If you know teens who are struggling with their trauma, it's important to let these teens know that you are there for support during this difficult time, whether by providing them with activities to prevent an panic attack or taking time to talk them through an attack. Teens who have experienced trauma are incredibly vulnerable and scared. Knowing that they have someone they can rely on during a difficult time can be just as valuable as any therapy.

Obsessive-Compulsive Disorder (OCD)

Another type of anxiety disorder teens can develop is obsessive-compulsive disorder (OCD). Known for its ritualistic behaviors, OCD can occur as early as childhood but can also manifest during adolescence. When teens experience OCD, not only are they dealing with reoccurring thoughts that upset them but they develop behaviors and habits in order to control them. In the definition of OCD, obsessions refer to the reoccurring thoughts which result in rituals or routines known as compulsions or compulsive behaviors.[4] Although there isn't a definitive explanation as to why people develop OCD, there is a strong possibility that teens may develop OCD if it runs in their family. However, some studies have found that OCD can manifest where communication errors occur in the front, back, and middle part of the brain. With OCD, signs can worsen over time, but they can also subside with time.

Signs of Obsessive-Compulsive Disorder

- Unable to control their thoughts and behaviors
- Do the same rituals over and over, such as hand washing, touching doorknobs repeatedly, repeating steps over and over again, organizing and reorganizing items, and so on.
- Don't like performing the rituals but help a teen cope with their anxiety.
- Rituals and routines can cause problems in a teen's life, such as chronic tardiness and losing friends because of his or her behavior

---

OCD can result in the loss of relationships as the disorder is exhausting and time consuming. There are several treatment options for OCD, which include psychotherapy and medication, but, as of now, there is no cure for this disorder. If you know teens who are struggling with OCD, let them know that you are here to help them get the help they need by guiding them to resources that can help them manage their anxiety.

MOOD DISORDERS

Depression and bipolar disorder are two types of the most common mood disorders. Mood disorders can occur in children, teens, and adults, but, notably, children and teens experience different signs from adults. Children are rarely diagnosed with a mood disorder, but teens often exhibit early signs that can be diagnosed and treated by a medical professional. Mood disorders can occur for a variety of reasons, including family history, medical conditions, history of substance abuse, and chemical imbalances in the brain. Although science has come a long way when it comes to psychiatric medicine and research, there is no definitive answer as to why mood disorders such as depression and bipolar disorder exist.

Depression

The most common mood disorder a teen can experience is depression. Depression has long been described as "feeling blue" or "down in the dumps" as a result of something that causes a person to be overwhelmed with sadness.[5] It's perfectly normal for all of us to feel down when something negatively affects us, such as losing a loved one or experiencing a bad breakup. While it's okay to have these feelings, they can become problematic when they start interfering with his or her life. The difference between feeling depressed and having depression is that teens who have depression experience chronic signs that prevent them from functioning—and hopefully have been diagnosed and are receiving medical attention for their depression. Signs of depression include but not limited to the following.

Signs of Depression

- Withdrawing from friends and family
- Having thoughts of hopelessness and extreme sadness
- No longer enjoying, or engaging, in activities they like
- Having difficulty paying attention or making decisions
- Having thoughts about being dead or wanting to be dead
- Feeling of worthlessness and/or guilt
- Not sleeping or eating well
- Body aches
- Having difficulty getting out of bed and feeling tired
- Grades are slipping or skipping class
- Abusing alcohol and drugs

When you think about mood, you often associate it with our current state of mind. In other words, when you say you're happy, sad, or angry, you often apply those feelings as your mood, which is why the phrases "being moody" or "being in a bad mood" exist. However, as people process their moods, and are able to shake off these moods, they can easily return to their day-to-day routines. When teens are diagnosed with a mood disorder, this means their moods are so severe that they are not able to continue their normal routines. For some, this disorder can be debilitating, which is why depression is classified as a mood disorder and requires medical treatment. To understand depression, not only do you need to understand the underlying causes, you must confront your own misconceptions and realize that your experience with depressed moods is not the same as someone who has depression.

If you witness teens experiencing any signs of depression, it's important to ask, or observe, how long these teens have been feeling this way and if the signs have been interfering with their daily activities. For example, has the teen missed school or other routine activities? Is the teen unkempt or uncommunicative? If these signs last longer than a few weeks, teens should seek medical attention. If medical attention is not sought, and teens start to experience more and more signs, for a prolonged amount of time, teens can develop major depressive disorder (MDD).

Although it can be difficult to differentiate the different types of depressive disorders and MDD, teens who are depressed typically experience low moods and low energy and can remain in that state for a time. Teens with MDD don't just experience sadness but their range of moods can shift from sadness to anger. Additionally, teens with MDD are at higher risk of substance abuse, self-harm, and suicidal ideation, and death by suicide. While depression can be managed with a combination of medication and psychotherapy, teens may experience more than one episode of depression throughout their lives. In other words, if a teen has an episode of MDD now, there is a possibility that he or she could experience another one within a few months or ten years from now, which is why it's important to help teens recognize their signs and guide them to resources to get them the help they need to live a productive and healthy life.

Bipolar Disorder

Bipolar disorder (formerly known as manic depressive disorder) is another mood disorder where teens experience a fluctuation between extreme moods, which are very different from their usual mood. Teens with bipolar disorder can experience an exaggerated state of happiness (manic episode) or a state of extreme sadness (depressive episode). Sometimes, teens can experience both a manic and depressive episode simultaneously, which is often categorized as a mixed episode. The major difference between bipolar disorder and depression is that teens must experience an episode of depression *and* mania in order to be diagnosed with bipolar disorder.

Signs of Bipolar Disorder

- Experience moments of increased energy
- Experience elevated moods (belief they are invincible and unstoppable)
- Experience moments of increased irritability
- Experience delusions of grandeur (i.e., believe that the CIA is chasing them or they can speak to angels)
- Engage in risky behavior (gambling, charging up credit cards, and having sex with multiple partners)

There are two types of bipolar disorder that teens can be diagnosed with. Classic bipolar disorder, or bipolar I, occurs when teens are in a depressive state but experience a manic episode. Bipolar I is also known for lying low in between episodes, which means a person can be in a manic depressive state that can last for six weeks, disappear, and return months, or years, later. Although teens typically don't experience signs of bipolar disorder until the late teens, or young adult years, it's also one of the hardest mood disorders to diagnose, as signs of mania often go undiagnosed. Why? Signs of bipolar I are completely different in adults than with teens. For teens with bipolar disorder, their moods change more frequently, their signs are more extreme, and they can possibly experience mixed episodes of mania and hypomania. In simpler terms, signs come and go, resolve themselves, and come back without any warning. However, if teens start exhibiting signs of suicidal thoughts or ideation, then these teens need help immediately as they are in danger of attempting suicide.

The second type of bipolar disorder, bipolar II, occurs when a teen has severe depression, but also experiences hypomania. When teens experience hypomania, they are much more subdued and experience very little irritability of agitation. Teens who are diagnosed with bipolar II rarely experience mania, but experts have confirmed that people with bipolar II suffer from extreme depression, which means they are susceptible of becoming addicted to alcohol and/or drugs or develop other mental health disorders. Although teens with bipolar II don't experience a full manic episode, they suffer from longer episodes of depression than teens with bipolar I.

Teens with bipolar disorder can live very productive lives if they seek out professional help to treat their disorder. Depending on their signs, and what the treatment plan is, teens can recover from their episodes with a combination of medication and psychotherapy. While there is no cure for bipolar disorder, there have been amazing strides in the last fifty years in treating this disorder, which is why it's important to emphasize to teens that there is nothing to be ashamed of if they are experiencing bipolar disorder.

Although it is not fully understood why bipolar disorders exist, experts have concluded that bipolar disorder can be attributed to family history, chemical imbalances in the brain, and traumatic events. Like with any other mental disorders, treating bipolar disorder is something that is going to take time, but not impossible. The best thing you can do for teens with Bipolar Disorder is inform them of their options and remind them that you are there to help them when they need it. Bipolar disorder can be one of the most difficult types of mood disorders to live with, but, through persistence, and support, teens can overcome their disorder and keep it at bay.

EATING DISORDERS

Along with depression and anxiety, eating disorders are fairly prevalent amongst teens and have devastating effects on the mind and body. Eating disorders occur when teens alter their eating habits to the point where they are dramatically decreasing, or increasing, their daily food intake through binge eating, vomiting, or fasting.[6] What might start out as an innocent attempt to lose five pounds in two weeks could develop into a habit that causes irreparable damage. What most people don't realize is that eating disorders often result from other problems. With most eating disorders occurring in teens, there is a high probability that teens have other mental health disorders, such as anxiety and depression. Eating disorders can also develop if a teen is abusing drugs or alcohol. The most common eating disorders include anorexia nervosa, bulimia nervosa, and binge eating.

Anorexia Nervosa

Prevalent among teen girls, anorexia nervosa, or anorexia, is closely tied to body image and beauty.[7] In the United States, numerous efforts have been made to celebrate beauty in all shapes and sizes. However, young women are constantly bombarded by images and products dedicated to ensure that they maintain a certain weight or look a certain way. At this point in their lives, teens are more vulnerable than ever to social pressure because they are wanting to be accepted for who they are and their bodies are also telling them that it's time to procreate. In most cultures, beauty and sexual maturity are often synonymous, which history has proven through the invention of corsets, codpieces, and bustles. Nowadays, beauty and sexuality continue to influence how young women look and what is desired in a mate; and, with the invention of Photoshop, social media, and the Internet, this force and the desire to control how one looks is even stronger.

Julia Bluhm's campaign that changed *Seventeen* Magazine

In 2012, an eighth grader named Julia Bluhm launched a petition through *Change.org* to demand that *Seventeen Magazine* stop altering the photo of their models because she grew very frustrated over the fact that her peers in her ballet were complaining about their weight. What started out as a simple petition for the magazine to publish one unaltered photos garnered more than 80,000 signatures worldwide and sparked a demonstration outside of the magazine's corporate offices.

According to NPR reporter Elsie Hu, "The barrage of correspondence from young girls led Ann Shoket, Seventeen's editor-in-chief, to invite Julia for a meeting and subsequently put out a new policy statement on the magazine's photo enhancements." Not only was this a major win for Julia Bluhm, her actions sparked young girls to speak up against false representation in beauty magazines like *Seventeen*. Also, right after Bluhm's victory, another online petition showed up demanding that *Teen Vogue* follow *Seventeen*'s example. To view this petition, log on to https://www.change.org/p/teen-vogue-give-us-images-of-real-girls.

If a teen comes from a culture where beauty and value depend on a tiny waist, these requirements can have a severe impact on the mental health of a teen. There is no one single cause of anorexia nervosa, but factors such as stress, peer pressure, lack of self-esteem can factor in to this disorder as well. Unfortunately, anorexia is not an uncommon disorder among teens. Although this disorder has been around for quite some time, it is even more prevalent as teens are constantly surrounded with images that dictate what they should look like, what they should eat, and how they should exercise. Furthermore, social media has given a faceless voice to critics who condemn young people by body shaming them to the point that teens can develop eating disorders such as anorexia.

Signs of Anorexia Nervosa

- Seeing themselves as overweight even if they are severely underweight
- Becoming obsessed with body image and developing routines to maintain that image, including portion control, eating specific foods, and how often they eat
- Engaging in behaviors such as binge eating, extreme dieting, excessive exercise routines, self-induced vomiting, and abuse dieting pills, laxatives, and diuretics
- Developing an intense fear or anxiety of gaining weight or becoming overweight

---

It's important to note that anorexia—that is, starving oneself—has a massive impact on the entire body. Teens can experience signs such as hair loss, muscle loss, and tooth decay. Over time, teens suffering from anorexia can develop serious health problems, such as heart failure, brain damage, anemia, osteoporosis, and infertility. Another problem with eating disorders like anorexia is if this disorder goes untreated, the more likely it will continue on into the young adult years, which usually ends in premature death. Sadly, anorexia kills more people than any of the mental health disorders, which is why it's important to know the signs, so you can help guide teens who are clearly in need of help.

The good news is that anorexia can be treated with the help of medical doctors, nutritionists, and therapists. The goal of the treatment is to help teens get past their negative thinking, get treatment for any other mental health disorders, and return to a healthy weight. Teens may be hospitalized based on the severity of the disorder as they may be suffering heart failure. Some may even be administered psychiatric drugs. Whatever the case, teens can recover and lead productive lives, which is why it's important they have access to resources and information to get the treatment they need.

Bulimia Nervosa

Similar to anorexia nervosa, bulimia nervosa is another eating disorder. With bulimia, the teen binge eats and immediately purges their body by inducing vomiting or purging their digestive signs using over-the-counter medications to prevent weight gain. When teens are diagnosed with bulimia nervosa, it means they feel they have no way to lose weight and will do everything they can from exercising, using laxatives, and diuretics. In other words, bulimics will do what they can to prevent an ounce of weight gain, which is incredibly dangerous to the body.

Bulimia is actually more common in teens than adults, and it is triggered by outside factors such as stress, trauma, or even dieting. As with the fasting of anorexia, binging is a way for a person to control their bodies in a world that is beyond their control, which is why experts attribute bulimia to factors like cultural standards, stress, and peer pressure.

Although teens experiencing bulimia often hide their disorder, they also tie their self-worth to their body image. As mentioned previously, bulimia often develops because of the beauty standard that young girls and boys are trying to achieve. Young people see images of men and women who are not only fit and slender but are a symbol of beauty, where looks can get everything from attention, money, love, and even happiness. These depictions have an impact on how teens view themselves, which can be incredibly stressful especially if the teens are being criticized for their weight or pressured by their peers to lose weight.

As with anorexia, bulimia can have devastating effects on the body, which include ulcers, pain, esophageal issues, and dental issues. Bulimia, if left untreated, can lead to heart failure and kidney failure. If you work with teens who you suspect might be bulimic, watch for these visible signs of this disorder.

Signs of Bulimia

- Eating a lot of food at one time
- Going to the bathroom after eating
- Physical symptoms of vomiting
  - Swollen and watery eyes
  - Scrapes or calluses on fingers (to induce vomiting)
  - Bloodshot eyes
- Excessive exercising
- May have symptoms of other mental health disorders, such as anxiety or depression

---

Teens diagnosed with bulimia can get treatment with the help of doctors, therapists, and nutritionists. There are a variety of treatments, such as cognitive-based therapy (CBT), which focuses primarily on why you do what you do and how it makes you feel. Either one-on-one sessions or group settings are offered to help manage the negative thoughts and behaviors. If these teens are suffering from another mental disorder, they may need medication to manage those signs as well. A nutritionist can help a teen develop healthy eating habits, which is important to restore nutrients and fluids that may have been lost.

Binge-Eating Disorder

Another eating disorder that affects teens is binge-eating disorder. Unlike anorexia and bulimia, binge-eating disorder does not include purging, nor does it include any aversions to food. Teens with binge-eating disorder are often overweight or obese as they are not trying to control what they eat, but feel they are out of control and just can't stop. Teens with this disorder tend to eat a lot of food, in a short amount of time, to the point they are uncomfortably full. These teens might experience a variety of physical and psychological signs that are not easy to see.

Signs of Binge Eating

- Obsessed, or sensitive, to their body image, food, and eating habits
- Don't eat around their peers
- Appear tired
- Rapidly gaining weight
- Feel guilty, or ashamed, after binge eating
- Feel extreme sadness, or distress, after binge eating
- Suffer from low self-esteem or experience depression or anxiety

---

As with other eating disorders, it is not understood why teens develop binge eating disorder, but there are factors that contribute to the disorder, such as mood disorders. It is not uncommon for these teens with binge eating disorder to also have depression; depression can trigger emotions that can force a teen to binge in the first place. Without treatment, teens with this disorder can develop serious health problems that have a massive impact on their bodies. In fact, people who are suffering from binge eating disorder are more susceptible to developing all sorts of medical issues, and suicidal ideation (thoughts of suicide) is common among this group. Treatment is available for this disorder, which may include the help of a psychiatrist, psychologist, a dietician, and/or therapist. If is the teens are also diagnosed with a mood disorder, they may be prescribed psychiatric drugs to help them feel better as well.

PSYCHOTIC DISORDERS

Of all of the mental health disorders, those that are often stigmatized, and misunderstood, are psychotic disorders. These disorders are often complicated, and no one really knows how they come to manifest, nor is there a cure. However, studies have revealed that most psychotic disorders stem from other health issues, such as substance abuse, neurological disorders, and infections. For teens, psychotic disorders typically don't develop until the late teens and early young adult years, but they may start exhibiting signs in the early teen years. Psychotic disorders are difficult to diagnose during adolescence because a lot of the signs mimic other mental health disorders, such depression and bipolar disorder. However, there are signs that a teen may be experiencing psychosis, which can develop from a psychotic disorder such as schizophrenia or bipolar disorder, where maniac episodes can trigger psychosis.

Psychosis

Psychosis is a symptom indicative of a psychotic mental health disorder. When psychosis occurs, teens may experience delusions and hallucinations that can severely impact their ability to function. There are five stages[8] in a psychotic episode that can vary in length, and it's not until the third stage that teens exhibit signs that clearly suggest they are experiencing psychosis.

Five Stages of Psychosis*

Stage One: Premorbid Phase (At Risk)

The person does not experience any symptoms but may be at risk for developing psychosis

Stage Two: Prodromal Phase (Becoming Unwell)

The person experiences some changes in his or her emotions, motivation, thinking, and perception or behavior. Whether or not the person is developing a disorder where psychosis can occur is still unclear.

Stage Three: Acute Phase (Feeling Unwell)

The person has symptoms such as delusions, hallucinations, and disorganized thinking and is unable to maintain relationships, work, and study.

Stage Four: Recovery

The person's individual process to attain a level of well-being.

Stage Five: Relapse

The person may only have one episode in his or her life or may go on to have other episodes.

*From *Youth Mental Health First Aid USA for Adults Assisting Young People*

If you suspect a teen might be developing a psychotic disorder, be aware that signs can gradually appear over time and may mimic other disorders such as bipolar disorder.

Schizophrenia

Schizophrenia is a mental health disorder commonly associated with psychosis that can appear in the late teen years. Schizophrenia is one of the most severe forms of mental health disorders as it is a chronic disorder with debilitating signs. Teens who experience schizophrenia experience three categories of signs: positive, negative, and cognitive.

Signs of Schizophrenia

Positive Symptoms (occur as a result of psychosis):

- Unable to distinguish reality from dreams
- Hear voices or see things that no one else can see
- Develop disorganized thought patterns or unable to express their thoughts in an organized manner
- Are extremely paranoid about people trying to hurt them
- Exhibit movement disorders where they repeat specific movements over and over

Negative Symptoms (occur when a teen experiences mood and behavior disruptions):

- Extreme mood shifts
- Talk in a monotone voice known as the "flat affect" or speak very little
- Unable to take pleasure in everyday life
- Unable to make friends

Cognitive Symptoms (affect a teen's ability to carry out important functions):

- Being able to process and comprehend information that is necessary to make decisions
- Unable to pay attention or focus
- Have trouble with using newly acquired information after learning it (i.e., the "working memory")

While there is no definitive answer as to why teens develop schizophrenia, studies[9] have shown genetics and environment may play a role as well as early brain development. Although it is not known which genes cause this disorder, it is becoming clearer that teens with a family history of schizophrenia may be prone to developing this disorder. As for environment, factors such as malnutrition, complications during, or after, birth, exposure to certain viruses, and psychosocial factors (developing coping skills) have been shown to be contributing factors to the development of schizophrenia.

In regards to treatment, teens do have options to manage their disorder with the help of medication (antipsychotics) and psychosocial treatments such as cognitive-based therapy (CBT) and substance abuse treatment. Teens who receive treatment are often able to live fulfilling lives, which is why it's important they have access to the care they need. If teens experience signs of psychosis, or schizophrenia, it does not mean they will become violent. Unfortunately, the stigma surrounding mental health disorders, especially schizophrenia, has led the general public to believe that people with schizophrenia are more apt to hurt others—this is not the case, although people with schizophrenia are at higher risk for hurting themselves. As a general fact, people with mental health disorders rarely become violent as their disorders tend to focus on the self rather than others.

Schizoaffective Disorder

Schizoaffective disorder is a type of mental health disorder where an individual experiences signs of psychosis, but doesn't necessarily meet the criteria of bipolar disorder, which, in this case, means teens don't experience a manic or hypomanic state. In other words, teens who experience a mood disorder and psychosis are candidates for schizoaffective disorder. Keep in mind, psychosis can also occur for other reasons such as substance use. Teens who use drugs or alcohol can experience a psychotic episode after use, but signs are only temporary. On the other hand, teens who experience signs of psychosis are more likely to use substances as a result of their disorder, which is one of the reasons why these teens should be encouraged to seek treatment.

SUBSTANCE USE DISORDERS

Substance use is not uncommon in adolescence. In the last few years, teens have taken experimentation to an all new level by huffing bath salts, ingesting hand sanitizer, and even ingesting detergent pods. While this behavior can be extremely dangerous, many teens will experiment with substances a couple of times for a variety of reasons, including peer pressure or to seek out attention. Although some may believe that teens behave like this because they are bored, or are just plain stupid, it takes more than a bored teen to want to put something in his or her body that could possibly kill the person.

Substance use can happen for several reasons. One reason teens use substances is mental illness, such as depression, bipolar disorder, PTSD, or anxiety. However, substance use can be a result of addiction as well. Again, teens may experiment with a variety of substances once or twice, but, when that use turns from recreational to dependence, these chemicals can cause serious harm to their brains and develop behaviors that include risk-taking, self-harm, and even suicide. If a teen becomes dependent on substance, he or she is prone to developing a substance use disorder such as alcohol use disorder (AUD), tobacco use disorder, cannabis use disorder (CUD), stimulant use disorder (SUD), and opioid use disorder (OUD).

Alcohol Use Disorder (AUD)

Alcohol is one of the most common substances that adolescents consume. Although teens are not legally able to purchase alcohol, some teens start drinking as early as 12 years old. In fact, the National Institute on Alcohol Abuse and Alcoholism (NIAAA) reported that youth 12 to 20 years old consume most of their alcohol by binge drinking. As to why teens consume alcohol, factors such as mental illness, abuse, stress, peer pressure, and family history can cause teens to develop substance use disorders.

Signs of Alcohol Use Disorder

- Bloodshot eyes
- Smell of alcohol on the breath
- Flushed complexion
- Unable to stand or walk straight
- Appear intoxicated
- Slurred speech
- Easily agitated
- Loss of friends
- Asking for money

What is alarming about alcohol use disorder is not just the effects it can have the body but the consequences of AUD, which can lead to death, incarceration, loss of family, loss of friends, and the inability to concentrate in school or gain meaningful employment. If you suspect teens to have AUD, ask them if they are okay and if they would like to talk. If you suspect that their disorder may be a result of abuse and/or mental illness, it's important to notify the authorities who can help them seek treatment. Common treatments for AUD can include rehabilitation, which is where teens are under the care of medical professions who will assist the teens with the withdrawal process. Teens should never be encouraged to quit "cold turkey" as withdrawal can be unbearable, and, in some cases, death can occur as the body may not be able to handle the process. Other treatment options are cognitive and group therapies, such as counseling and/or attending group meetings similar to Alcoholics Anonymous (AA)s. If a teen is using alcohol as a means of self-medicating because of a mental illness, a doctor may prescribe them medication to manage their mental disorder as well.

Tobacco Use Disorder (TUD)

Just like alcohol, teens experiment with tobacco as a result of peer pressure or they see it as a way to appear cool and mature. In fact, vaping among teens is very popular because it has been marketed as a better alternative to cigarettes as they smell better and taste better. However, science has recently revealed that vaping is actually more dangerous. Whether it's smoking cigarettes or consuming smokeless tobacco, teens who continue to use tobacco are at risk for developing serious health problems, such as respiratory disease, gum and tooth disease, heart disease, lung disease, and cancer. Teens who have mental disorders are more susceptible to TUD as they use it as a means of self-medicating.

Signs of Tobacco Use Disorder
- Smell like cigarette smoke on breath and clothes
- Have shortness of breath
- Chronic coughing
- Yellowing of teeth

If you suspect some teens using tobacco, it's important they are made aware of the effects it can have on their health and, if they feel they can quit, inform them they can get treatment from a medical professional. Treatment options for tobacco use include cognitive therapies, support groups, and medication. There are popular smoking cessations that can be purchased over the counter, but, depending on how young the teen is, it is best to ask a doctor about the use of these products as a teen's body chemistry is very different from that of an adult. Other alternatives such as hypnotism and mindfulness have helped people overcome smoking, but, again, any kind of treatment needs to be discussed with a medical professional.

Cannabis Use Disorder (CUD)

Marijuana, aka Cannabis, is one of the most common drugs used by teens. Known for its mind-altering effects, teens who use marijuana are at higher risk of developing respiratory and lung problems and the possibility of developing brain abnormalities. However, CUD is very common among teens who have mental disorders. While there is debate among experts as to whether cannabis causes mental disorders, there is also evidence that teens may be using cannabis as a means of self-medicating for a mental disorder.

Signs of Cannabis Use Disorder

- Red or bloodshot eyes
- Unable to concentrate
- Changes in behavior
- Smell of marijuana on clothing and breath
- Changes in appetite
- Appear sleepy

While there is no evidence as to whether or not marijuana can cause major health problems like cancer, the effects of cannabis can leave a teen unable to concentrate either at school or work. The greatest cause for concern with cannabis is that it can affect a teen's ability to drive, which could cause an accident that can kill the teen or an innocent bystander. There are currently no treatment options for cannabis use as science has not proven cannabis to be addictive. The best way to treat cannabis use is for a medical professional to determine if this use is a cause of an underlining disorder.

Stimulant Use Disorder (SUD)

The most popular substance associated with SUD is *methylenedioxymethamphetamine otherwise known as Ecstasy*. Known for its hallucinogenic properties, Ecstasy, or "E" or "MDMA," alters the brain chemicals known as Serotonin, Dopamine, and Norepinephrine that are responsible for regulating emotions ... regulating emotions, body temperature, and heart rate. Teens can ingest Ecstasy either in pill or powder form. What's important to note is that MDMA is the purest form of Ecstasy; whereas, the pill form might contain other substances that could kill a teen. In addition to Ecstasy, other substances including: amphetamines, methamphetamines, and cocaine can have similar effects on a teen's body.

Signs of Stimulant Use Disorder

- Experience hallucinations
- In a state of euphoria
- Heightened sexual urges
- Enhanced energy
- Experience intense hot and cold flashes

Since this substance alters the chemical responsible for regulating emotions, teens can develop mental health challenges from prolonged use. Treatment for SUD is still in development, but with the help of a medical team, you can help a teen figure out what the next steps are. With most substance use disorders, patients who have developed a dependency usually go through a detox process under close supervision. Depending on the reason a teen is using ecstasy, such as a mental disorder, they will be treated for that disorder as well as substance use.

Opioid Use Disorder (OUD)

Opioid use, specifically prescription opioids, has become a growing problem in the United States. Reasons why teens use prescription opioids is they are looking for a way to get high or use it for pain management. The main problem with prescription opioids is they are easily accessible as teens can take them from their parents' medicine cabinet or get them from friends and family members. The most dangerous aspect of prescription opioid misuse is that teens may not realize that dosages are based on specific criteria. For example, weight determines dosages and strength. Second, if teens don't know the ingredients, they may have a severe allergic reaction. Lastly, substances may have side-effects that teens may not be able to handle, especially if ingested with alcohol, which can result in death. Among the most misused prescription drugs are opioids like Vicodin, Oxycodone, and Codeine, which, if used for a prolonged amount of time, can become addictive.

Signs of Opioid Use Disorder

- Experience loss of energy
- Have restricted pupils
- Changes in behavior
- Loss of friends
- Poor coordination
- Confused or easily agitated if confronted
- Not sleeping

One of the treatment options for opioid use disorder is a method called medical-assisted treatment (MAT), where patients are administered medications under the care of a medical team. The most common medications used to treat opioid dependence is Methadone and Buprenorphine, which helps with the withdrawal signs. Like the other substance use disorders, teens misusing opioids may have a mental disorder. Along with MAT, teens should be evaluated for mental illness as they may be self-medicating with opioids, which will require additional treatment.

DISRUPTIVE BEHAVIOR DISORDERS

Disruptive behavior disorders develop when teens experience chronic behavior problems. These behaviors often include bouts of anger, hostility, and defiance. These disorders can occur for a number of reasons including the following:

- Abuse
- Genetics
- Substance use
- Problems at home

Disruptive Behaviors Disorders and Attention-Deficit Disorder (ADHD)

Disruptive behavior disorders can coexist with other disorders, but, more so, with attention-deficit hyperactivity disorder (ADHD). According to Children and Adults with Attention-Deficit/Hyperactivity Disorder (CHADD),[10]

> About 40 percent of individuals with ADHD have oppositional defiant disorder (ODD). ODD involves a pattern of arguing; losing one's temper; refusing to follow rules; blaming others; deliberately annoying others; and being angry, resentful, spiteful and vindictive.
>
> Among individuals with ADHD, conduct disorder (CD) may also be present, occurring in 27 percent of children, 45–50 percent of adolescents and 20–25 percent of adults with ADHD. Children with conduct disorder may be aggressive to people or animals, destroy property, lie or steal things from others, run away, skip school or break curfews. Adults with CD often exhibit behaviors that get them into trouble with the law.

While disruptive behavior disorders can coexist with ADHD, it's important to know the signs of ADHD. ADHD can appear in youth as young as three years old, where children can exhibit hyperactivity, impulsivity, and inability to pay attention. Teens who have been diagnosed with ADHD can experience the following:

- Difficulty paying attention
- Easily distracted
- Unorganized
- Lose, or misplace, things frequently
- Unable to complete tasks that require effort

Although these behaviors are not uncommon with young children, teens who exhibit these behaviors may have ADHD as it not only affects their ability in school but explains why he or she has trouble making friends, completing his or her homework assignments, or listening to authority figures. Teens can be diagnosed with ADHD based on this criterion, but only a mental health professional can make that call as a teen will need to undergo an assessment. The good news is that ADHD can be managed with the help of a medical team and medication (if necessary).

Oppositional Defiant Disorder (ODD)

Oppositional defiant disorder is a disruptive behavior disorder that often coexists with ADHD. According to CHADD: The National Resource on ADHD, "[a]pproximately one-third to one-half of all children with ADHD may have coexisting oppositional defiant disorder (ODD). These children are often disobedient and have outbursts of temper."[11] Teens with ODD will often lose their temper with adults and have extreme fits of anger and irritability. In addition to losing their temper, teens with this disorder see authority negatively, which explains why they often argue with adults, refuse to obey orders, and even take their anger out on others if they make a mistake. While it's easy to confuse ODD with ADHD, the difference between these behaviors is that teens with ODD often feel angry and resentful. Just like ADHD, teens with ODD can manage their disorder with professional help, which may include therapy and/or medication.

Conduct Disorder (CD)

Conduct disorder is another disruptive behavior disorder where teens exhibit aggressive behaviors. Just like ODD, "Conduct disorder may occur in 25 percent of children and 45 percent of adolescents with ADHD. CD is more commonly seen in boys than girls and increases in prevalence with age." Teens with CD are often prone to fighting, bullying, assaulting, stealing, or engaging in risky behaviors, such as using drugs and alcohol.

In addition to these behaviors, teens can also be promiscuous and pressure others into sex. It is not uncommon for teens with CD to have trouble in school and at home as their disorder triggers reactions that make it difficult for teens to sustain healthy relationships. However, teens can manage their CD with professional help and, if necessary, medication. It is imperative that teens stick with their treatment plan to keep their emotions in check.

SELF-HARM

Self-harm occurs when a teen experiences such an intense amount of pain that he or she physically injures oneself. There are various forms of self-injury, such as cutting, burning, punching objects and person, hair pulling, piercing their body with sharp objects, and even breaking limbs. Self-harm is not exclusive to teens as it can occur to anyone at any age; however, self-injury is more common among females than males.

One reason why teens may engage in self-harm is they are desperate for relief. Teens who feel this kind of pain typically do not know how to express themselves, which is why self-harm becomes a type of coping mechanism. Another reason why teens may harm themselves is they feel lonely and want to be noticed either by their friends or family. Self-injury can also occur because they are trying to cope with a traumatic event they experienced or they feel so detached from everything around them. While self-injury could be a result of a mental disorder, self-harm can be a way for teens to declare control over their own bodies and as a means to prove something to their peers. For teens, the most common form of self-harm is cutting, which involves the use of sharp objects such as razors, knives, and other sharp objects that can puncture the skin.

If you notice a teen is cutting or otherwise hurting himself or herself, it's important to let the teen know that he or she is not alone and that the teen can get help. Treatment for cutting, and other self-harm, could include cognitive behavior therapy and medication. Furthermore, if the self-injury is a result of mental disorder, teens may receive additional treatment, which can help alleviate some of the pain they may be feeling. Although there is no cure for self-harm, it's important to inform teens that there are alternatives to harming themselves, such as channeling their emotions into healthy activities such as art, music, physical activities, and mindfulness activities (i.e., meditation).

MENTAL HEALTH DISORDERS AND TEENS WITH AUTISM SPECTRUM DISORDER (ASD)

According to the *DSM-V*, neurological disorders such as autism, or autism spectrum disorder (ASD), are another type of mental disorders. Autism is a brain-based disorder that impairs a person's ability to communicate, socialize, and may cause him or her to develop repetitive behaviors. ASD can appear as early as three years old. At age three, children should be mobile and communicating with caregivers. Children who have not hit these developmental milestones may be exhibiting signs of ASD. Luckily, there are early interventions that can help children with ASD develop the skills they need to lead a productive life.

Is Autism Spectrum Disorder a Mental Illness?

This has been a hotly contested topic among mental health professionals and Autism support networks. Dr. Matthew Rettew (2015) states, "[t]his debate has surfaced many times before and in many venues. It is a difficult one to resolve because there really is no scientific basis on which to separate a psychiatric disorder from a neurological or developmental one."[12] From a scientific point of view, autism is considered a mental health disorder simply because it takes place in the brain. Common signs of ASD include the following:

- Delayed speech
- Aversions to certain sights, sounds, textures, and taste
- Flap their hands, clap their hands, and rock back and forth
- Unable to maintain eye contact
- Repetitive behaviors and speech
- Obsessions over their favorite things
- Unable to read body language and social cues
- Don't like to be touched or don't understand the concept of personal space
- Have difficulty managing change especially in daily routines

However, given the stigma that surrounds mental health challenges, there are many misconceptions regarding ASD—just because a teen has autism, it doesn't mean he or she will automatically develop other mental health disorders. Of course, just like their neurotypical peers, teens with ASD can develop disorders such as depression and anxiety as a result of genetics and environment.

Since most mental health disorders typically manifest in the early young adult years, signs of mental health disorders start appearing in the early adolescent years as the brain is undergoing a set of changes that can trigger signs of mental disorders. However, it should be noted that children as young as five years old can develop PTSD as a result of trauma or as an effect of their parents' trauma. Like most adolescents, teens with ASD can develop other mental health disorders, which can occur for the same reasons that neurotypical teens develop anxiety and depression.

Teens with ASD and Mental Disorders

One major difference between teens with ASD and neurotypical teens experiencing a mental health disorder is that teens with ASD may have more difficulty expressing themselves. If a teen is on the lower end of the autism spectrum and has severe disabilities (i.e., not being able to talk or move), he or she will not be able to communicate how one is feeling versus a teen on the higher end of the spectrum. Furthermore, teens with ASD are aware that they are different from their peers, which can lead to feelings and behaviors that might trigger other mental disorders, such as anxiety and depression.

Behavior is key in recognizing if a person is experiencing a mental disorder. If teens start exhibiting behaviors that are completely opposite of their normal behavior, this is usually a sign that they may be experiencing a mental disorder. This is true even among teens with ASD as any deviation can disrupt daily routine and result in a meltdown. In other words, if teens with ASD are unable to enjoy the things they like or do not have the energy to do the things they like to do, then this can result in multiple outbursts, which signal that the teen is experiencing a mental disorder.

Teens with ASD experiencing a mental disorder can get treatment in the form of medication, therapy, and social interventions. More importantly, teens with ASD need guidance during this time as they are not only coping with a body that's changing but also experiencing symptoms that affect the way they feel, physically and emotionally. If you work with a teen with ASD and notice a significant change in his or her behavior, it's good to communicate this with the teen's caregivers and parents. Furthermore, remind staff that outbursts can occur with teens with ASD. As long as the teen isn't hurting oneself, or others, you can help teens regulate their behavior by remaining calm, asking simple and direct questions, and offering them a quiet place to calm down.

Although it may be particularly difficult for teens with ASD who are experiencing mental health challenges, the good news is that they can get treatment to manage their behaviors. Again, there is no cure or explanation as to why some teens develop mental disorders, but modern medicine and practices have helped millions of people manage their disorders and to lead a happy and productive life. As teen advocates, and mentors, you can be a part of the support network teens need to cope with their mental health disorder. By taking the time to learn what mental disorders are, what they look like, and what can be done to help teens experiencing these challenges, you can better serve our teen patrons.

NOTES

1. "What Is Mental Illness." American Psychiatric Association. https://www.psychiatry.org/patients-families/what-is-mental-illness.
2. "Five Major Mental Disorders Share Genetic Roots." National Institute of Mental Health. March 1, 2013. https://www.nimh.nih.gov/news/science-news/2013/five-major-mental-disorders-share-genetic-roots.shtml.
3. "Anxiety Disorders." *National Institute of Mental Health.* https://www.nimh.nih.gov/health/topics/anxiety-disorders/index.shtml.
4. "What Causes OCD." BeyondOCD.org. http://beyondocd.org/information-for-individuals/what-causes-ocd.
5. Mondimore, Francis Mark, and Patrick Kelly. *Adolescent Depression: A Guide for Parents.* Baltimore: Johns Hopkins University Press, 2015. 71–75.
6. Bakewell, Lisa. *Mental Health Information for Teens: Health Tips about Mental Wellness and Mental Illness, Including Facts about Recognizing and Treating Mood, Anxiety, Personality, Psychotic, Behavioral, Impulse Control, and Addiction Disorders.* Detroit: Omnigraphics, 2014.
7. "Statistics." National Institute of Mental Health. October 23, 2017. https://www.nimh.nih.gov/health/statistics/prevalence/eating-disorders-among-children.shtml.
8. Kitchner, Betty Ann, and A. F. Jorm. Youth Mental Health First Aid USA: For Adults Assisting Young People. Baltimore: Mental Health Association of Maryland, 2012.
9. "Genetic Study Provides First-Ever Insight into Biological Origin of Schizophrenia." Broad Institute. September 12, 2016. https://www.broadinstitute.org/news/7823.
10. CHADD. "Coexisting Conditions | CHADD." CHADD—The National Resource on ADHD. http://www.chadd.org/Understanding-ADHD/About-ADHD/Coexisting-Conditions.aspx.
11. CHADD. "Disruptive Behavior Disorders | CHADD." CHADD—The National Resource on ADHD. http://chadd.org/understanding-adhd/about-adhd/coexisting-conditions/disruptive-behavior-disorders.aspx.
12. Rettew, David. "Is Autism a Mental Illness?" *Psychology Today.* October 8, 2015. https://www.psychologytoday.com/us/blog/abcs-child-psychiatry/201510/is-autism-mental-illness.

ADDITIONAL READINGS

Books

Bakewell, Lisa. *Mental Health Information for Teens: Health Tips about Mental Wellness and Mental Illness, Including Facts about Recognizing and Treating Mood, Anxiety, Personality, Psychotic, Behavioral, Impulse Control, and Addiction Disorders.* Detroit: Omnigraphics, 2014.

Diagnostic and Statistical Manual of Mental Disorders: DSM-5. Arlington: American Psychiatric Association, 2013.

Hu, Elise. "*Seventeen* Magazine Takes No-Photoshop Pledge after 8th-Grader's Campaign." NPR. July 6, 2012. https://www.npr.org/sections/thetwo-way/2012/07/05/156342683/seventeen-magazine-takes-no-photoshop-pledge-after-8th-graders-campaign.

Mondimore, Francis Mark, and Patrick Kelly. *Adolescent Depression: A Guide for Parents.* Baltimore: Johns Hopkins University Press, 2015.

Purkis, Jeanette, Emma Goodall, and Jane Nugent. *The Guide to Good Mental Health on the Autism Spectrum.* London: Jessica Kingsley Publishers, 2016.

Websites

National Alliance on Mental Illness (NAMI)—https://www.nami.org/
National Institute of Mental Health—https://www.nimh.nih.gov/index.shtml
Mental Health America—http://www.mentalhealthamerica.net
Substance Abuse and Mental Health Services Administration—https://www.samhsa.gov/

3

◇ ◇ ◇

BEING PREPARED FOR TEEN MENTAL HEALTH CRISIS

When a teen experiences a mental health crisis, it can be traumatic for the teen and for everyone who loves and care for him or her. Mental health crises can happen to anyone at any time, which is why it is important to recognize the signs. It is also vital to have the tools necessary to assist and support a teen during the crisis. While no one can truly be prepared for a mental health crisis, you can do things to learn how to manage a crisis. Does that mean you have to get a degree in psychology? Not at all. However, there are resources you can access that offer basic help for someone to get the care they need. Think of yourself as a facilitator in the process.

ONLINE MENTAL HEALTH RESOURCES

To better understand mental disorders, it's important you take the time to research the causes and signs of mental disorders. Although there are more definitive and extensive resources available to better explain mental illness, this book should give you a good start. As a teen librarian, you have no qualms about research, but mental illness research probably seems more daunting. Remember, the most difficult part about researching mental illness is at the beginning. Even researching mental health disorders can be overwhelming, but the following online resources are a great place to start, since they are literally at your fingertips.

American Psychiatric Association (APA)

http://www.apa.org/

The American Psychiatric Association is an organization made up of psychiatrists who are devoted to caring for patients with psychiatric disorders. While most of you are familiar with APA-style formatting, APA's mission is to provide the hundreds of thousands of psychiatrists with support, set high standards of quality care, and advance the field of psychiatric medicine through research. While this organization is mainly supportive of medical professionals, it provides educational material for patients and their families.

APA is also responsible for publishing the *Diagnostic and Statistical Manual of Mental Disorders* (2013), which provides researchers and clinical professionals with information to diagnose mental disorders. While this text is lengthy, and not an easy read, it is authoritative, as it organizes and defines the various types of mental disorders. If your library has a copy, take a look at it as it can come handy if you need a better understanding of why depression is considered a mood disorder and not a behavioral disorder. To get a copy of the *DSM*, visit: https://www.psychiatry.org/psychiatrists/practice/dsm.

When you log on to APA's website, it's easy to navigate as you have options to choose from. The section that will interest you the most is "Topics." When you click on this heading, you will see a list, A to Z, of mental disorders. By clicking on a topic, you will be directed to other pages that have simple definitions, additional research topics, and how you can get help. While this resource doesn't list all the signs of the mental disorder, which is detailed more in the *DSM*, it does have some helpful tips on where to get help. In addition to the resources that the APA offers professionals, it does provide a wealth of information for patients and family members via its website at www.psychiatry.org.

If you are interested in learning more about treatment options, APA provides a variety of examples, which have been proven successful. Please keep in mind that treatment for mental disorders varies among patients and that teens need to work with their medical team to develop a treatment plan. In other words, the examples provided by the APA are just examples and, in some cases, guidelines for physicians to follow to develop a treatment plan.

National Alliance on Mental Illness (NAMI)

https://www.nami.org/

The National Alliance on Mental Illness (NAMI) is a nationwide organization that advocates for people suffering from mental illness. As one of the biggest nonprofit mental health organizations, NAMI has accomplished a lot in bringing awareness to the needs of people suffering from mental illness. Since NAMI's resources are vast, they may be able to provide library staff with training or information sessions about mental illness. In fact, I was able to contact my local chapter, via Facebook, and even invite a speaker to present on mental illness to teens.

In comparison to the website provided by the American Psychological Association, NAMI's website is much more thorough and provides users with information ranging from knowing signs of mental illness, treatment options, advocacy issues, policy making, support for families, and other topics related to destigmatizing mental illness. The section that will help the most is the "Learn More" section as it contains the following information:

- Knowing the warning signs
- Mental health conditions
- Mental health by numbers
- Treatment; research
- Infographics and fact sheets
- Public policy

All of these topics provide a lot of information that is not only relevant to your education but can be shared with teens who ask about mental illness.

Another section of the website that is worth taking a look at is "Find Support," as there is a section specifically for teens and young adults. One of NAMI's goals is to help people advocate for their own mental health. This particular section does exactly that, as it provides teens with tips and tools on how to recognize mental illness and where to get help. As you review this section, take a look at the other topics that help teens who may have a friend with mental illness, manage mental disorders in college, and even provide suggestions on how to make friends while managing a mental illness. All of this information is useful not just for you but for teens as well, so be sure to remember this resource in the event a teen, or his or her parents, needs this information.

Along with its advocacy efforts, NAMI offers a variety of programs that include education classes for parents, support groups for individuals with mental illness, peer-to-peer classes, and community education programs. These offerings help provide a better perspective on people living with mental illness. From my own experience working with NAMI, they employ volunteers and members who are passionate about helping people with mental health challenges, which makes them the ideal resource and a potential partner to bring awareness to staff and the communities.

National Institute of Mental Health (NIMH)

https://www.nimh.nih.gov/index.shtml

As a U.S. federal agency dedicated to researching mental disorders, the National Institute of Mental Health (NIMH) offers a wealth of information that anyone can access at any time. Given the complexity of mental disorders, this resource provides an online database filled with easy-to-read articles, statistics, and resources for people with mental disorders. Furthermore, NIMH has an outreach program where it partners with mental health organizations to bring information to every community. In fact, every state has partnered with NIMH, and you can reach out directly to these partners to bring research-based materials or have a volunteer present on these findings to bring awareness to staff and communities.

Although their information is geared toward medical professionals, you can also order, or download, their free *Consumer Health Publications*. What is great about these publications is they provide all members of the community with information and suggestions to assist teens experiencing a mental disorder. These publications are available in various formats such PDF and ePub. You can also order hardcopies of these publication, provided NIMH has them in stock. Lastly, some of this information is available in Spanish, which is helpful if your library serves a large Latino population. Here is a list of their publications you can order or download:

For Parents:

Autism
　　https://www.nimh.nih.gov/health/publications/autism-
　　　spectrum-disorder/index.shtml
Bipolar Disorder in Children and Teens
　　https://www.nimh.nih.gov/health/publications/bipolar-dis
　　　order-in-children-and-teens/index.shtml
Helping Children and Teens Cope with Violence and Disasters:
　　What Parents Can Do
　　https://www.nimh.nih.gov/health/publications/helping-children-
　　　and-adolescents-cope-with-violence-and-disasters-parents/
　　　index.shtml

For Teens

NIMH Answers Questions about Suicide
  https://www.nimh.nih.gov/health/publications/nimh-answe
  rs-questions-about-suicide/index.shtml
Teen Depression
  https://www.nimh.nih.gov/health/publications/teen-depression/
  index.shtml
The Teen Brain: Six Things to Know
  https://www.nimh.nih.gov/health/publications/the-teen-brain-6-
  things-to-know/index.shtml

TEEN-FOCUSED ONLINE RESOURCES

Medline Plus-Teen Mental Health

https://medlineplus.gov/teenmentalhealth.html
Medline Plus is a public librarian's best friend when it comes to providing patrons with mental health information. What makes this consumer health resource great is that it provides teen-focused resources that are easy to understand and use. Whatever your level of knowledge is in regard to mental disorders, this resource starts with the basics and evolves to more elaborate topics for those of you who want to learn more. Furthermore, Medline Plus connects teen researchers with other resources such as the National Institute of Mental Health (NIMH) and the Substance Abuse and Mental Health Services Administration (SAMHSA) that leads the nation on mental disorder research. Although this resource is meant for teens, library staff can learn from it as well since it encompasses quite a bit.

TeenMentalHealth.org

http://teenmentalhealth.org/
TeenMentalHealth.org, another resource focused on teen mental disorders, developed by Dr. Stan Kutcher, TeenMentalHealth, is dedicated to improving teen mental health through scientific research to develop programs and resources in collaboration with health care providers, policy makers, schools, nonprofit organizations, business owners, and even the public. What is amazing about this organization is that all of its resources, publications, and reports are available free of charge, which means you can download and print these resources to share with your colleagues.

TeenMentalHealth.org provides students and advocates with mental health information that explains the various mental disorders, understanding teen behaviors, and how sleep and injuries can affect a teen's brain. All of this information is presented in a simple and easy-to-understand way. Along with these resources, TeenMentalHealth.org provides customized materials to assist friends, parents, educators, and health care professionals to help teens experiencing a mental disorder. Keep in mind that the data provided by TeenMentalHealth.org comes from Canada, but the information is solid so feel free to print out or share these resources to weblinks, collections, and social media.

TRAINING ON MENTAL DISORDERS

While it is important to learn about mental disorders through reading and research, trainings can also be critical, as they offer you the opportunity to speak with an expert who can provide insight and answer any questions you may have. Trainings come in a variety of forms, from formal in-person trainings, webinars, and online classes, to informal conversations with community health organizations. Although some trainings can be pricey, there are often ways to get funding for those trainings through either grants or sharing the cost of those trainings with neighboring library system or with city/county departments. When it comes to working with people in need, costs should not hinder you from getting the training you need to help the youth, which is why it's so important to rely on resources that already exist. Furthermore, as public library staff members, you have another invaluable resource at your fingertips, which is your local public health department.

City/County Public Health Departments

As a librarian, you will likely meet people, teens and adults, who have mental disorders, so be sure to familiarize yourself with your local public health department. They will have the resources and services that can assist these individuals. Although the level of services varies from region to region, it's important that you reach out to make it known that you work with and serve people with mental disorders and that the library may not know how to assist someone in crisis. Although the perception of public libraries has changed from quiet places filled with books to centers of community engagement, many local agencies may not realize that you serve everyone regardless of their ability, race, religion, identity, and mental state.

By connecting with your local public health department, you are creating a relationship that has the potential to not only increase the library's presence but help make the public more aware of these services. Furthermore, in your library's role as centers for community engagement, you actually have the ability to connect organizations to one another, which is a great show of interdepartmental cooperation and a good way to educate and/or train staff.

Mental Health First Aid USA

Think of Mental Health First Aid as CPR for those who are experiencing a crisis. In the event of a crisis, this training gives you the tools to support someone during a mental health crisis. As a mental health first aider, you *are not* responsible for giving medical or professional advice but to simply assist someone until professional care can be administered. Mental Health First Aid is an eight-hour training that provides learners with mental health literacy to either assist themselves, or others, experiencing a mental health crisis. Mental Health First Aid provides training focusing on both adults and youth, which is important to have as teens may show early sign of mental illness before a mental health disorder manifests.

During this training, you will learn to recognize signs of mental health disorders and provide practical advice on how to approach and assist a young person in need. Mental Health First Aid also provides a trainer program, where individuals attend a more extensive training and they will be prepared to train others in Mental Health First Aid, which is an ideal course to take so you can train not only our staff but fellow agencies and even educators.

Like most intensive trainings, there is a cost to these trainings, which may make it difficult for some library systems to participate. However, if this is a service that is desperately needed and our departments, and other departments, would like to participate, then there are grant opportunities available through Substance Abuse and Mental Health Services Administration (SAMHSA). For more information on how to get Youth Mental Health First Aid Certification, visit

Mental Health USA
https://www.mentalhealthfirstaid.org/take-a-course/course-types/
    youth/
1-888-244-8980, ext. 4
Hours: Monday–Friday 8:30 AM–5:00 PM ET

LIBRARY MENTAL HEALTH INITIATIVES

Libraries all over the country have made a significant effort in ensuring their patrons have access to mental health services. Whether it's through roving community health services or providing mental health first-aid trainings for staff, libraries have taken a proactive approach to assisting people with mental illness. The goal for these initiatives is to provide more services for people experiencing mental health challenges, staff training, reduce the need for calling 911 in an emergency, and educating the community about mental health and how the library can help them. What's even more extraordinary about these initiatives is the impact they have had on staff and patrons. Lastly, these initiatives have helped to change the perception that libraries aren't just old buildings with books, but a place where you can get help to live a healthy, happy life.

San Francisco Public Library Social Worker Program

After the economic collapse in 2008, the number of people experiencing homelessness increased to where 15 percent of the library's patrons didn't have permanent housing. In 2009, the San Francisco Public Library hired its own full-time social worker with one mission: help those experiencing homelessness get the help they need to get off the streets and into permanent housing. When Leah Esguerra was hired, she not only made it her mission to help those in need but wanted to change the perception of homelessness in the library.

The library is one of the very few places patrons experiencing homelessness can use as a means of shelter and safety, but, the public started to make complaints about this population using the library. After realizing the number of patrons in need, Esguerra decided to hire individuals experiencing homelessness to serve as consultants. By hiring these individuals, Eguerra has been able to change the perception of the library and its population of individuals experiencing homeless. According to Esguerra, in an interview with Juli Fraga (2016), "these programs are humanizing homelessness throughout the library . . . [and] the library becomes a sanctuary for many of the patrons and our program helps them to feel safe again."[1]

Along with her team and the San Francisco Homeless Outreach team, Esguerra provides patrons with assessments and referrals for mental health services, housing services, and case management. The main focus of this program revolves around empathy and how libraries can provide safety and sanctuaries for those who don't have a home to go to. More importantly, employing people who were once homeless is an authentic way of helping individuals, as these team members empathize with those who need help. As of 2016, 150 patrons have found permanent housing and 800 have enrolled in social and mental health services.[2]

Pima County Library Nurse Program

Another mental health initiative that has had a significant impact on its community is the Pima County (AZ) Library Nurse Program. The reason why the Pima County Library wanted to develop a mental health initiative is because the main library serves a high population of people experiencing homelessness, mental illness, and poverty. Given these conditions and because of the 2008 recession, access to mental health services was in danger and the library decided that it needed to hire a social worker.

Just as the San Francisco Public Library collaborated with the San Francisco Public Health Department, the executive leadership team of the Pima County Library wanted to connect with the Pima County Public Health Department. After much discussion, the Pima County Library decided that a public health nurse was a better alternative. According to Johnson, Mathewson, and Pechtel (2014), a public health nurse (PHN) provides the following:[3]

- Services tailored to the specific population
- Nursing assessments
- Case management
- Public health education

In 2010, the Pima County Library and the Pima County Public Health Department were able to create a library nurse program, which provided a qualified individual with a full-time position located inside the library. Along with working with patrons, the library public health nurse would provide oversight of the entire program and assist staff and security in the event of an emergency. Also, as stated previously, the library public health nurse would also conduct assessments, make referrals, and provide care for those who needed. In 2012, the Pima County Public Library hired its first library public health nurse.

While the library public health nurse program was desperately needed, it became apparent that the caseload was too much for one person to handle as the person was traveling between the library's six branches. After reevaluating the responsibilities of the nurse, and the position, the library decided to divide the 40-hour-a-week position into 5 library public health nurses. After one year, the public health nurse program reduced the amount of 911 calls by 26 percent. As of today, the program is still in effect and won the library several accolades, including the 2013 Top Innovator Award by the Urban Library Council and the 2014 American Public Health Associations' Lillian Wald Service Award. In addition, two of the public health nurses were recognized as Tucson's *Fabulous 50 Nurses*.[4]

California State Library Mental Health Initiative

In 2016, the California State Library received federal funding to launch a mental health initiative to help train library staff who work with patrons with mental disorders. The goal of the initiative is to provide trainings, including a mental health first-aid trainer program, free webinars focusing on mental disorders, and a series of mental health videos. The best part of this initiative is one of its focus was on serving teens with mental disorders.

Through this component of the initiative, library staff was invited to attend four free webinars, focusing on youth mental illness and trauma informed care. During the 2017–2018 grant year, library staff will have another opportunity to participate in a mental health first-aid trainer program, additional webinars focusing on LGBTQ mental health issues, de-escalation strategies, mental health first-aid trainings focusing on specific communities (Spanish-speaking, public safety personnel, and older adults).

Along with these webinars, library staff also has access to training videos that focus on promoting a positive staff culture about mental health, what to do and what not to do when interacting with patrons with mental illness, establishing positive relationships with disruptive patrons, exploring compassion fatigue, and addressing customer complaints from patrons with mental illness.

FUNDING FOR MENTAL HEALTH TRAININGS

The Substance Abuse and Mental Health Services Administration (SAMHSA), a division of the United States Department of Health and Human Services, is the only federal department that strives to significantly reduce the impacts of substance use but is also dedicated to bringing awareness to mental illness by providing services and opportunities for the nation to advocate for those in need.

As the only federal agency dedicated to take the lead on mental health education, SAMHSA has a wealth of resources available to those who are interested in learning more or knowing how they can help their community. Along with educating the public about mental health, SAMHSA participates in many campaigns that cover everything from community dialogue, substance abuse prevention, trauma informed care, programs for people experiencing homelessness, to training opportunities for underserved communities. Along with these resources, SAMHSA also offers grant opportunities for organizations to provide resources for their community in regard to mental health advocacy and treatment. In fact, in 2014, SAMHSA provided grant funding for Mental Health USA's Now Is the Time Initiative, where 119 state and local educational agencies received mental health first-aid training as a result of school violence. If libraries are interested in applying for SAMHSA grants, know that it will take some time, as there are numerous grants to research and the application process will be just as lengthy. Also, keep in mind that funding can change so be sure to apply as soon as possible.

NAVIGATING A TEEN MENTAL HEALTH CRISIS

When it comes to mental health crisis, it's important to remember it is just as serious as any other health crisis. If teens are exhibiting physical signs that indicate any kind of self-harm (i.e., cuts, overdose, and/ or signs of extreme fear or paranoia), professional help is needed immediately. However, if a teen is expressing thoughts of suicide, you need to be able to distinguish whether thoughts are just thoughts or if these thoughts will become actions. In the event staff is unable to obtain Youth Mental Health First Aid certification, through Mental Health First Aid USA, there are steps you can take to listen, assess, and take action when necessary.

Legality of Assisting Teens with Mental Disorders

As mentioned earlier, the role of library is rapidly changing in our communities and libraries are often the last place for some to get help, and the only safe haven for others. For teens, libraries are more than places to study; in fact, libraries have become a sanctuary for teens, where they can study, hang out with their friends, and, for some, get something to eat and a place to stay safe. All teen patrons have a story, which is why you should be prepared for anything, especially a mental health crisis. With education and training, it's important to find out what your legal obligations are for helping a teen in distress.

Unlike medical professionals and educators, *library staff members are not obligated to report or step in unless the teen is in immediate danger*. If a mental health crisis were to occur in our buildings, knowing who is certified in mental health first aid is crucial, as these individuals have the knowledge to support a teen during this difficult time. If you do become a certified mental health first aider, you will be integral in coordinating an emergency in the event of a crisis. If teens under the age of 18 require medical attention, it's important to involve their parents as they can get their teen help. However, if the teen discloses abuse at home, either at the hand of a parent or relative, the mental health first aider will need to report this to proper authorities, who will make the decision if a parent should be involved. If a teen is not experiencing a crisis but is exhibiting obvious signs of distress, the mental health first aider should notify the parents and explain to the teen that he or she needs help and the teen's parents can get him or her what the teen needs. If no one in your building is certified to handle these kind of situations, the next best thing is to call the paramedics, as they are trained, and equipped, to respond to a crisis.

Library Policies and Procedures

In order to help a teen during a crisis, the library should have policies and procedures in place to assist staff. While most libraries have behavior polices that outline what behaviors will not be tolerated in the library, it is important to add, or revise, statements that provide a little leniency for individuals experiencing mental illness. Along with these policies, it's important that every patron has access to these standards, which is why they should be on display or strategically placed where everyone can read them. In addition to their placement within the library, make sure the rules are clearly stated, easy to read, and should be updated periodically as times change. Be sure to include the consequences for violating library policies as we want to ensure that everyone has a pleasant and safe experience in the library.

When revising library polices, propose a clause that makes reasonable accommodations for patrons with mental illness. For example, if a patron has a mental health crisis in the library, propose an appeal process to reinstate library privileges based on disability. More importantly, educate staff that a mental illness qualifies as a disability based on the criteria set by the American Disabilities Act (ADA), which defines "disability as a physical or mental impairment that substantially limits one or more major life activities."[5] By having this clause in your policies, not only can you prevent a major lawsuit; you are providing teens with mental illness with an opportunity to use the library without having to fear the behavior will get them into trouble.

Along with revising policies, provide crisis procedures for staff. When developing these procedures, invite your public health department to assist. With a set of procedures in place, the staff not only have instructions on how to handle a mental health crisis but also have a clear set of guidelines as to what they have to do (i.e., connecting a patron with emergency services or ask for a staff member with mental health first-aid training for assistance) and what they are expected not to do, which is diagnosed and treated. Furthermore, these procedures can protect staff in the event a patron accuses staff for not adequately handling a situation or in the event someone gets hurt. In the following table are some tips you can include in your procedures.

Developing Procedures for a Teen Mental Health Crisis

In the event a social worker, or mental health first aider, is not available to assist a patron in distress, policies can instruct staff on how to assist a patron who is in distress. Here are a few tips you can include in your policies to help the staff de-escalate a situation or provide further instruction as to when the authorities need to be involved:

When approaching a patron during a mental health emergency, do the following:

- Stay calm and approach the person slowly.
- Ask a colleague to assist if you feel you need the support.
- Keep an arms-length distance between you and the patron.
- Stay calm and listen carefully.
- Be respectful and take their concerns seriously.
- Watch your facial expressions and body language.
- Ask simple and direct questions.
- Don't try to solve their problems.
- Keep your emotions under control.

In the event a patron wants to hurt themselves:

- Call your police department or dial 911.
- Listen carefully to the dispatcher's instructions.
- Clear the area around the patron to ensure his or her safety and the safety or your patrons.
- When help arrives, follow their directions or stay near in the event they need information.

After the emergency:

- Alert your supervisor as soon as possible.
- Take a moment to calm down and refocus.
- Fill out the appropriate paper work or incident report.

Again, you are not legally obligated to step in. If the staff feel they are able, and willing to assist, they at least have the knowledge on how to serve and assist a patron with mental illness.

WORKING WITH LOCAL
COMMUNITY RESOURCES

Another great resource you can utilize in an emergency is your city or county public health department. Within most health departments, there are social workers who may be able to assist teens in distress. Why rely on your public health department? Unlike Mental Health First Aiders, clinical social workers have the training and the certification to provide professional assistance to those who may be experiencing a mental health crisis. By reaching out to the public health department and informing them that you have patrons suffering from mental disorders, you can ask the department to deploy their clinical social workers to assist the staff. Libraries in California, Arizona, Denver, Ohio, and Canada are starting to hire social workers to focus on library patrons experiencing mental health issues.

These resources are just a few of many other resources available in your community. To educate yourself, and your fellow colleagues, you need to go into your community and find out what is available. If you are able to establish a partnership with your local public health department, they can help you connect with other organizations that provide mental health services. Also, get input from your staff and colleagues as they may be able to point you to organizations that can provide training at little to no cost. Again, while training opportunities may require a lot of coordination, the benefits outweigh the negatives as you are not only forming partnerships but also providing staff with valuable information to help them advocate for teens in need.

NOTES

1. Fraga, Juli. "The Social Workers Humanizing Homelessness at the San Francisco Public Library." CityLab. March 29, 2016. https://www.citylab.com/life/2016/03/humanizing-homelessness-at-the-san-francisco-public-library/475740/.
2. Schmerl, B. "How the San Francisco Public Library Is Helping the Homeless." *Reader's Digest*. July 29, 2016. https://www.rd.com/true-stories/inspiring/library-helping-homeless/.
3. Johnson, Kenya, Amber Mathewson, and Karyn Prechtel. "From Crisis to Collaboration: Pima County Public Library Partners with Health Department for Library Nurse Program." Public Libraries Online from Crisis to Collaboration Pima County Public Library Partners with Health Department for Library Nurse Program Comments. February 28, 2014. http://publiclibrariesonline.org/2014/02/from-crisis-to-collaboration-pima-county-public-library-partners-with-health-department-for-library-nurse-program/.
4. "Library Nurse." Pima County Public Library. https://www.library.pima.gov/public-health-nurse/.
5. "Mental Health Conditions in the Workplace and the ADA." ADA National Network. May 2, 2018. https://adata.org/factsheet/health.

4

◇ ◇ ◇

ASSISTING TEENS DURING A MENTAL HEALTH CRISIS

When a teen is in crisis it can be stressful and frightening for everyone—especially the teen in crisis. Not only is the teen dealing with emotions he or she doesn't understand but the teen can experience extreme physical pain or paranoia. For adults working with teens with mental illness, it's vital they know that anything can happen during a crisis, which is why it's important to know when to step in and how. While it's helpful to have a certified mental health first aider in every library, the reality is that not every library is able to afford the training or even want to take on this responsibility. If this is the case for your library, familiarize yourself with the signs of a crisis and learn how you can help support a teen during this difficult time.

HOW TO RECOGNIZE A MENTAL HEALTH CRISIS

A mental health crisis occurs when a teen is unable to control his or her thoughts and feelings that can cause extreme distress. Depending on the mental disorder, there are signs teens may exhibit that can result in physical harm or even death. If a teen is suicidal, he or she may be showing signs that include drastic changes in appearance and thoughts of despair. A panic attack includes physical symptoms fueled by anxiety. If you know the teens you work with, you can probably tell if their behavior indicates a mental health crisis. For teens you don't know well, other warning signs can help you assess if they are in distress and in need of help. Please note that not all teens will respond, or want, your help during this difficult time. Nevertheless, knowing how to support them will help them in one way or another.

Tips to Approaching a Teen in Crisis

If you see a teen in distress, pay attention to his or her behavior. If the teen appears to be in pain, or seems fearful, there is a chance he or she may be experiencing a crisis. Other signs can include the following:

- Extreme paranoia
- Severe anxiousness
- Unable to regulate his or her breathing or hyperventilating
- Agitation
- Unresponsive or appear catatonic
- Rocking back and forth or uncontrollable movements
- Uncontrollable crying

If teens appear to have any of these warning signs, notify a colleague that you suspect something is happening and you may need assistance.

Depending on the crisis, the teen's safety, your safety, and the safety of your patrons is important as you won't know what the teen is thinking or feeling. Once you have alerted help, walk over to the teen and ask him or her, in a calm and respectful manner, if he or she is okay. If the teen responds and says he or she is not okay, sit down with the teen and ask what's going on and why the he or she feels so. Also, let the teen do most of the talking if the teen can. Why? There is a possibility that teens haven't fully comprehended their thoughts, and, by talking about these thoughts, they may be able to figure out why they are feeling this. In some cases, teens may have never had the opportunity to really talk about why they want to die, which is why you need to actively listen to everything they are saying.

Tips for Active Listening

- Attempt to make eye contact but be mindful that eye contact may not be appropriate based on the teens' culture or abilities
- Be empathetic and respectful.
- Be mindful of your facial expressions and tone (don't roll your eyes or don't make unnecessary noises).

- Do not judge or shame a teen by saying, "You need to get over it" or other people have it worse."
- Be careful with your language (i.e., using stigmatizing language such as "crazy" or "psycho").
- When teens say something you don't understand, it's okay to ask the teens to clarify what they are saying.
- When discussing how the teens are feeling, talk about ways to help them with their problems.

When speaking with a teen who is extremely vulnerable and scared, take extra care with your facial movements and reactions. Be sure to listen, and react, nonjudgmentally as teens may retreat into their shells if they sense you are insincere. As the teen discusses what's going on, be sure to assess if the teen is danger of hurting oneself. If you sense that the teen is in danger, call 911 immediately. If you are certified in mental health first aid, administer first aid right away; otherwise, keep talking to the teen to find out more about what he or she is feeling as help is on the way.

Assisting Teens Who Are Suicidal

If a teen expresses feelings of suicide, it's important to know the following symptoms:

- Withdrawing from family and friends
- Using drugs or alcohol
- Feeling hopeless or saying they are better off dead
- Threatening to hurt themselves
- Researching ways to kill themselves
- Giving away their possessions
- Saying goodbye to their friends or family

If a teen is exhibiting any or all of these signs, you need to ensure that you and the teen are safe before giving care. If you believe the teen has a weapon, notify the proper authorities and explain that the teen intends to die by suicide. Once you have assessed whether or not the teen has a weapon, you need to ask the teen if he or she is feeling suicidal. For example, you might say something like:

"Sometimes, when people get so overwhelmed and stressed out, they feel like they want to die. I've noticed some changes in you and want to ask you do you feel like ending your life?"

When you approach a teen in distress, it is crucial for you to remain calm. As difficult as it is, you want to ensure the teen feels safe talking to you. If you start to panic, you may inadvertently frighten the teen or he or she may take it as an act of judgment, which is the exact opposite of what is needed. If the teen doesn't respond to your questions, let the person know you are concerned about him or her and ask the teen—directly—if he or she feels like killing oneself or have thoughts of suicide. If the teen says he or she is not really serious about killing oneself, don't just blow it off. Take the teen's behaviors seriously as he or she might feel ashamed for feeling so and may not feel comfortable talking about it.

There is a myth that if you ask teens if they want to die by suicide, you are putting the idea into their head. According to the director of the *Youth Depression and Suicide Prevention Research Program*, Cheryl A. Kind (2016, p. 36), "[o]ne study examined the impact of responding to research questions about suicidal thoughts on students and found no negative effects (Gould et al., 2005). Another study examined the impact of such questions on individuals recently discharged from a psychiatric inpatient service and found they were rarely associated with increased self-harm (Eynan et al., 2014)."[1] When asking teens if they have thoughts of suicide, know that you are not putting them in danger, but also let them know that these thoughts are not a sign of weakness nor are they uncommon. Reassure the teen that many people have had these thoughts and that help is available to control these thoughts.

In the event the teens do not admit they are suicidal, be sure to remain calm as you find out if they have a plan and how they plan to kill themselves.

When Teens Appear Suicidal

If a teen discloses his or her intention to die by suicide, ask if he or she has a plan by asking the following questions:

- Can you tell me more about your plan?
- Are you committed to killing yourself? If so, do you have a date and time?
- Have you thought about how you would kill yourself?
- If you could change how you feel, would you consider not killing yourself?

These questions are never easy. In fact, no one ever wants to ask these questions, but, for the sake of the teen in distress, you need to find out how serious the teen is about dying by suicide. If you believe the teen is committed to carrying about his or her plan, call 911 and stay with the teen until help arrives.

One thing to remember about teens who have thoughts of suicide is they may not actually be suicidal. Although it sounds contradictory, suicidal ideation is not the same as crafting and planning to die by suicide. If a teen does not have a plan or doesn't express the intent to die, encourage the teen to get professional help. Whether it's giving them phone numbers to hotlines, contact information for local adolescent psychiatric care, or resources about their feelings, teens need to get help right away, especially if they are feeling suicidal. Moreover, by asking these questions, you will be able to assess how realistic this threat is and if you need to call for help immediately.

Not every discussion you have with teens who may be suicidal will be the same. In fact, some may never reach the planning stage. The most important thing to remember is that these conversations are vital in figuring out the teens' true intentions and help them get the help they need. As a teen advocate, you need to show the teens that they are not alone. More importantly, you want to help them help themselves by demonstrating how to get the information they need. In the event of a crisis, it is helpful to have a list of resources readily available at our information desks or lead teens to our collections and/or sections dedicated to mental health.

Once the teen has calmed down, or asks for help, the next thing you need to ask is if the teen's parents are aware of his or her feelings. If the teen doesn't want to tell his or her parents, remind the teen his or her parents can get the help needed. If a teen reveals that his or her thoughts of suicide are related to problems at home, alert the proper authorities who can legally intervene and get the teen the care he or she needs. If the teen continues to refuse help, and is adamant about killing oneself, you need to call 911 immediately. After calling for help, explain to the teen you care about him or her and want him or her to be safe. Although the teen may see this as a betrayal of his or her trust, you are doing the right thing to keep that teen safe and alive.

As a librarian, you are not responsible or obligated to diagnose and treat teens with mental illness. Assisting teens during a crisis is not the same as diagnosing or treating. In offering to help teens during a crisis, you are simply seeking to support, encourage, and get the teens the help they need. While some of you may not feel comfortable with approaching teens in a crisis, know that your courage and dedication can help them out of crisis and into the arms of professionals who can help them get better. You can literally be a lifeline for teens who don't have anyone else they can talk. If you are willing, and ready, to assist teens who are suicidal, know they will never forget you and will appreciate what you have done.

To learn more about suicide prevention, here are some great resources to consult:

Anxiety and Depression Association of America, ADAA. "Suicide Prevention: Tips for Kids and Teens." https://adaa.org/learn-from-us/from-the-experts/blog-posts/suicide-prevention-tips-kids-and-teens.

NASP: The National Association of School Psychologists. "Preventing Youth Suicide: Tips for Parents & Educators." https://www.nasponline.org/resources-and-publications/resources/school-safety-and-crisis/preventing-youth-suicide/preventing-youth-suicide-tips-for-parents-and-educators.

National Institute of Mental Health. "Suicide Prevention." https://www.nimh.nih.gov/health/topics/suicide-prevention/index.shtml.

Substance Abuse and Mental Health Services Administration. "Preventing Suicide: A Toolkit for High Schools." HHS Publication No. SMA-12-4669. Rockville, MD: Center for Mental Health Services, Substance Abuse and Mental Health Services Administration, 2012.

Turner, Erlanger A. "Understanding Teen Suicide: Tips for Prevention." *Psychology Today*. June 13, 2018. https://www.psychologytoday.com/us/blog/the-race-good-health/201306/understanding-teen-suicide-tips-prevention.

Assisting Teens Experiencing a Panic Attack

Teens who experience a panic attack are literally experiencing an overwhelming amount of stress that can trigger physical symptoms and can make them ill. If you have ever experienced a panic attack, you know it can be scary. However, there are ways to keep a panic attack at bay by developing coping mechanisms or, in the case of a severe panic attack, medication is prescribed by a medical professional. Teens who experience panic attacks can be sent into a frenzy, which is why it's essential to know the signs of impending panic attack, which can include the following:

- Sweating
- Shaking and trembling

- Shortness of breath
- Chest pain
- Feeling faint
- Numbness
- Extreme fear of dying
- Extreme paranoia

If you think a teen is having a panic attack, talk to the teen to see if he or she has ever experienced a panic attack before. If the teen has had these attacks before, it's important to ask the teen about any coping mechanisms he or she uses to help him or her calm down. If this is the first time the teen is experiencing a panic attack, it's important to stay calm and ask the teen if he or she would like us to help them. Depending on the teen's symptoms, it may be necessary to call 911 especially if a teen loses consciousness. Here are a couple of techniques you can use to help a teen process the panic attack:

- Provide teens with a quiet place to settle down.
- Ask the teens to lean, or sit, against the wall so they have stability.
- Let the teens know these feelings are momentary and will pass soon.
- Stay with them as they calm down.
- When they are calm, ask them if they would like us to call for help or contact their parent.

Just as with teens who are experiencing thoughts of suicide, you need to be supportive, calm, and respectful as teens get through their attacks. Also, remember to listen to teens when assisting them. If teens say they are experiencing chest pain and want you to call for an ambulance, pick up the phone and call an ambulance. The last thing you want to do is exacerbate the attack by assuming what the teens need and not actually listening to what they want. Once the teens have gained their composure, ask the teens if they want you to call for help. If not, let the teens know there are treatment options available to manage their attacks and that they should notify their parents or caregivers so they can get professional help they need. In fact, provide the teens with information resources about panic attacks and what they can do to prevent or manage an attack. Here is additional information for teens about managing a panic attack:

Daniels, Natasha. *Anxiety Sucks!: A Teen Survival Guide*. North Charleston, SC: CreateSpace, 2016.
Kissen, Debra, Bari Goldman Cohen, and Kathi Fine Abitbol. *The Panic Workbook for Teens: Breaking the Cycle of Fear, Worry & Panic Attacks*.

Oakland, CA: Instant Help Books, an Imprint of New Harbinger Publications, 2015.

McDonagh, Thomas, and Jon Patrick Hatcher. *101 Ways to Conquer Teen Anxiety: Simple Tips, Techniques and Strategies for Overcoming Anxiety, Worry and Panic Attacks*. Berkeley, CA: Ulysses Press, 2016.

"Panic Disorder." *Teen Mental Health*. http://teenmentalhealth.org/learn/mental-disorders/panic-disorder/.

Puckett, Lily. "Do THIS the Next Time You Have a Panic Attack." *Teen Vogue*. May 25, 2017. https://www.teenvogue.com/story/panic-attacks-how-to-calm-down.

Willard, Christopher. *Mindfulness for Teen Anxiety: A Workbook for Overcoming Anxiety at Home, at School, and Everywhere Else*. Oakland, CA: Instant Help Books, An Imprint of New Harbinger Publications, 2014.

Assisting Teens Experiencing Psychosis

When a teen experiences a psychotic episode, there are steps you can take to help the teen. As mentioned before, you learned that people who experience psychosis are more susceptible to hurting themselves than others. However, if a teen is experiencing hallucinations or delusions, it's imperative that you remain calm. If you are not sure if the teen is experiencing psychosis, here are some warning signs:

- Experiencing hallucinations (i.e., seeing, hearing, and smelling things that are not there);
- Exhibiting behaviors such acting disruptively or talking to themselves
- Having delusions (i.e., believing or saying something or someone is out to get them)

If you notice a teen in this type of distress, stay calm and approach the teen slowly and deliberately. When asking questions, keep your sentences short and simple, and make sure you leave space between you and the teen. Depending on the severity of the episode, clear the area of patrons in the event a teen lashes out. If the teen is in extreme distress, call 911 rather than trying to de-escalate the situation yourself. As you listen to the teen, try to be as positive and encouraging as you can, as the teen might be fearful.

As you listen, try not to judge or "fix" the teen, keeping in mind that psychosis is incredibly complex. Also find out if the teen has thoughts of suicide. If the teen answers yes, find out if he or she has a plan and assess if the teen is in real danger. If not, ask the teen if he or she has experienced this before and if the teen has any coping mechanisms to help the teen calm down. Although psychosis can come out of nowhere, it can occur when a teen stops taking his or her medication or be induced by other substances. If you feel a teen is under the influence of drugs and/or alcohol, pay attention to signs of intoxication and have the teen sit against a wall in case he or she loses consciousness. Again, you are not obligated to figure out why the teen is experiencing psychosis, but, if you are willing, you can use any of these tips to assist the teen experiencing psychosis.

When the teen calms down, ask if you can call his or her parents or caregiver. Always let teens know there is nothing to be ashamed or embarrassed. Also, let teens know there are treatment options and offer them a list of resources. If you are not able to help the teen calm down, call for help immediately. When the emergency medical team arrives, be sure to relay what the teen is experiencing and let the teen know that these people are here to help him or her. Try and stick around if you can so the teen can see you but give the emergency medical team plenty of space and be ready to answer any questions they have.

Assisting Teens Who Experience a Drug/ Alcohol Overdose

If a teen comes into the library and is exhibiting signs of alcohol and drug overdose, there are steps you can take to determine if the teen is in danger. Signs of an overdose include the following:

- Dilated pupils
- Shallow breathing
- Loss of balance
- Weak or slow pulse rate
- Experiencing psychosis
- Experiencing paranoia
- Excessive sweating or clammy skin
- Appearing agitated

Before approaching the teen, remain calm and be slow and deliberate in your movements. If the teen is hallucinating, or agitated, quick movements can scare the teen, which could exacerbate his or her condition. As you approach the teen, ask direct questions like:

- Do you need help?
- Did you take something to make you feel this way?
- How much did you take?
- Are you hurting or having trouble breathing?

Before asking questions, make sure the teen is conscious. If the teen starts losing consciousness, call 911 right away and stay by the teen's side until help arrives. If the teen is going in and out of consciousness, air on the side of caution and call for help as substances take time to metabolize in the teen's body.

After calling call 911, be sure the teen is in a position or an area free from sharp objects such as desks, chairs, and bookcases in case the teen loses consciousness. If the teen has a seizure, let the seizure pass and immediately turn the teen to side to keep his or her airway open. If the teen does seize, call for help immediately. Once the emergency medical team arrives, be sure to explain all the symptoms the teen is experiencing and if they identified the substance he or she used.

What Happens during a Seizure

There are several types of symptoms a person can experience during a seizure that include, but not limited to, the following:

- Clenching of the jaw
- Jerking movements
- Frothing at the mouth
- Biting of the tongue
- Loss of consciousness
- Loss of bodily function
- Screaming
- Confusion and/or agitation

Assisting Teens Who Are Harming Themselves

While self-injury can only be diagnosed by a physician, if you think a teen might engaging in self-injury, there are several things you can do to assist the teen. First of all, don't assume that a teen who is hurting themselves is trying to kill oneself. Raychelle Cassada Lohmann, MS, LPCS (2012), states that "[self-harm and suicide] oftentimes get grouped together because both are inflictions of pain and sometimes people who begin with self-harm may later commit suicide. Generally, people who self-harm do not wish to kill themselves; whereas suicide is a way of ending life."[2] Teens who engage in self-harm are looking for ways to cope with their feelings and, by inflicting pain, they feel relief. If you suspect the teen is harming oneself, you can help by expressing your concern for him or her and asking if he or she needs help.

Before approaching teens who are hurting themselves, observe their present condition. If they are experiencing any of the signs that indicate the possibility of an overdose, call for help right away. If not, remain calm, and start a conversation with them by asking a few questions.

- "I've noticed you have had several injuries recently and I was wondering if you could tell me how they happened?"
- "I've noticed cuts on your (arms, legs, hands, face, etc.) and just wanted to see if you're okay."

When talking to teens about their injuries, be respectful and don't stare at their injuries. Self-injury is extremely embarrassing for a teen, so be sure not to stare. If teens reveal why they are hurting themselves, don't try to advise or condemn their behavior as they are already vulnerable. Instead, talk to them about other ways to relieve their pain. More importantly, ask them if you can help them find help, and, if necessary, call for emergency medical attention. Self-injury, more often than not, can be a result of an underlying mental disorder. Mental Health America notes that "self-injury behaviors can be a symptom of other mental illnesses such as: personality disorders (esp. borderline personality disorder); bipolar disorder (manic depression); major depression; anxiety disorders (esp. obsessive-compulsive disorder); and psychotic disorders such as schizophrenia."[3]

Assisting Teens Who Are Aggressive

If a teen exhibits signs of aggression, there are several things you need to know. First, aggression in teens can be a result of other behaviors, such as substance use, and/or associated with disruptive behavior disorders, such as ADHD, oppositional defiant disorder, or conduct disorder. Secondly, teens who become aggressive may have experienced a traumatic event in their life and don't know how to manage their emotions. Thirdly, aggression can occur when a teen becomes frustrated. When this frustration boils over, the teen can resort to violence to relieve that stress.

With behavior disorders, anything can set the teens off if they don't know how to manage their feelings. In the event a teen becomes agitated, or aggressive, there are several steps you can take to help the teen calm down or diffuse a difficult situation. The first step is to evaluate whether or not you can help the teen. If the teen is having an episode and you don't feel safe approaching the teen, call for assistance or 911. If the teen is feeling agitated, always make sure there is space between you and the teen.

As you speak with teens, never ask them to calm down as this may aggravate them even further. Keep calm and watch the volume of your voice as teens may misconstrue your tone as antagonizing. When asking questions, ask teens if you can help them or ask if they have coping mechanisms to help them calm down. Depending on how well you know the teens, ask them to talk about something that makes them feel good to help them regulate their behavior.

If you suspect a teen is aggressive due to substance use, observe his or her behavior and see if the teen is in danger of an overdose. If teens exhibit signs of intoxication, as well as aggression, call for help right away as teens might not be able to control themselves while under the influence.

SELF-CARE AND DEBRIEFING A CRISIS

Assisting teens in crisis can be an incredibly stressful event for you, for your staff, and even your patrons. Once a crisis is resolved, take a moment to step away and get some fresh air. De-escalating a crisis can be traumatic, so be sure to pay attention to your body and what it is saying to you. If you feel like you're going into shock, call for assistance either from your colleagues or from the paramedics. Either way, get to an emergency room right away as shock can be fatal, depending on your symptoms. If you just need to take a walk and calm down, that is okay. Also, if you feel like every nerve in your body is fried, it's okay to ask for the day off and come back when you are calm and relaxed. Whatever helps you come back to your center, it's important that you always take care of yourself after every crisis, so treat and be good to yourself.

When you are ready to dive into your incident reports, be as thorough as possible. While it's good to have a detailed report for the record, writing down all the steps you took can help formulate a plan in the event this happens again. Once you complete your report, share it with every staff member in the event they have questions or might want to know how to assist someone. This would also be a good time to ask your mangers if it would be possible to get first-aid training from your public health department. It's better that your entire team is confident and prepared to respond to these emergencies as these crises are not exclusive to teens but adults as well.

NOTES

1. King, Cheryl A. "Asking or Not Asking about Suicidal Thoughts: The Possibility of 'Added Value' Research to Improve Our Understanding of Suicide." *Monitor on Psychology*. July/August 2016. http://www.apa.org/monitor/2016/07-08/ethics.aspx.
2. Cassada Lohmann, Raychelle. "Understanding Suicide and Self-harm." *Psychology Today*. October 28, 2012. https://www.psychologytoday.com/us/blog/teen-angst/201210/understanding-suicide-and-self-harm.
3. "Self-injury (Cutting, Self-Harm or Self-Mutilation)." *Mental Health America*. August 17, 2016. http://www.mentalhealthamerica.net/self-injury.

5

◇ ◇ ◇

CREATING A TEEN MENTAL
HEALTH INITIATIVE

As a teen librarian, you know that teens can be passionate, loyal, and hard working. However, one of the biggest challenges in being a teen librarian is having to explain to the public, and even to coworkers, why teen services is so important and why teens deserve to have a place, and even a say, in library services. As you have already read, mental disorders are a significant issue among teens and they can have a significant impact on a teen's life and his or her ability to live a productive life. Now that you have a better understanding of common mental disorders, and how you can assist teens in distress, it is important to raise awareness about mental health by providing resources and services that teach teens how to advocate for their own mental health and for those they know and care about. In order to accomplish the goals, consider launching a teen mental health initiative.

So what exactly is a teen mental health initiative? A teen mental health initiative is declaring to the community that the library is dedicated to supporting teens with mental illness by providing services, resources, and programs to assist teens in need. Whether it is about providing teens access to mental health–themed books, giving out mental health brochures, or developing a safe space, the library's teen mental health initiative can take on any form as long as it meets the needs of teen patrons. More importantly, you want to allow the initiative to grow and evolve, as it will be providing a service that is not normally found in most libraries. Lastly, a teen mental health initiative is about giving a voice to teens. If a teen has a mental disorder, this initiative should be about supporting the teen in his or her time of need, while encouraging their peers to advocate for community mental health education.

WHY BUILD A TEEN MENTAL HEALTH INITIATIVE?

As the role of library evolves, not everyone is willing to embrace these changes. One of the biggest concerns voiced by the staff is "we're librarians . . . not social workers." As mentioned before, to help teens with mental health issues, you do not have the same training or responsibilities as licensed clinicians, who have the ability to diagnose and treat. However, as information specialists, you already have the skills to help patrons find what they are looking for. Further, as a public servant, if a patron asks for assistance, you help him or her to the best of your ability or refer the patron to resources that can answer those questions. This is standard procedure for librarians, which is why building a teen mental health initiative is not as radical as it seems.

While the library has the capacity to supply information to the public, librarians have the skills to navigate information requests and to educate and lead the public to what they are looking for.

If a patron approaches the desk looking for books or articles about thyroid disease, you would look up this information in the library catalog or databases. If you still can't find exactly what the patron is looking for, peruse trustworthy medical websites such as the World Health Organization (WHO), Johns Hopkins Medicine, Mayo Clinic, or Centers for Disease Control and Prevention (CDC). These same procedures can be used to build a teen mental health initiative, which is why libraries have this incredible opportunity to assist a group of teens who need help the most.

In order to create the foundation of the teen mental health initiative, you need to think about the following:

- Why should the library focus on teen mental health?
- Would a teen mental health initiative draw these teens to the library?
- How would the teen community embrace this initiative?
- Who else would be supported by this initiative?

- What would you want to include in this initiative?
- How will the community benefit from this initiative?

By identifying key points that support a teen mental health initiative, you will have the guidance you need to move forward. Once you lay the foundation for your initiative, the next step is to reach out to your teen community. Why? When you invite teens to help build library services, it gives an opportunity for them to see you in action and what it means to be a librarian and, through this invitation, teens can create impactful library services where their passion and dedication can support an initiative based on their ideas. While the goal of the initiative is to support teens with mental health or disorders, this project can inspire and provide teens with an opportunity to build empathy while learning to advocate for teens in need. Moreover, teens will get real-life experience to help them develop into leaders for change, which, in itself, is a massive accomplishment for the library and the community.

Proposing the Teen Mental Health Initiative to Library Management

Before launching any type of mental health programs and services, secure support from your supervisor and upper management. By presenting the need for teen mental health services and resources, you can point out important facts and feedback that prove the need for these services. More importantly, if you can, provide administration with an overview that will demonstrate how the library can help teens in the community and how it can become a valuable community resource where teens can get help simply by going to the library. Depending on the size of your system, speaking with a director might prove difficult, so first pitch the idea to your supervisor. Whatever the answer may be, in regard to supporting the initiative, introduce it in stages to prove the need for these services and its success. Here is one way you can pitch this idea:

- Research statistics about teen mental health and present those statistics either in a presentation or in a report.
- Let your administration know that mental illness does not typically manifest until the young-adult years, which means teens can get help now to prevent future mental health episodes.
- Discuss your interactions with teens when it comes to mental illness.

- Discuss what your local public health department is providing the community and mention the possibility of partnering with them to provide mental health services.
- Discuss what other mental health services are available to bring training resources and public services into the library.
- Inform your administration that this mental health initiative will provide teens with an opportunity to build empathy and leadership skills, which are essential to teen development.
- Introduce the types of services and resources that you would like to see in the library.
- Discuss how you will support the staff through this process and who will assist in this planning process.

By identifying the evidence that supports the need for a teen mental health initiative, and how the library can support and promote other city services, you can convey your management that a teen mental health initiative supports the ideology that libraries are more than just books—it's about caring and supporting its most vulnerable.

Educating and Supporting the Staff

Encountering, and serving, patrons experiencing mental health challenges is not a new phenomenon in libraries. In fact, librarians have been serving all kinds of patrons for years, but that doesn't necessarily mean that the staff is properly trained or equipped for handling these interactions. In order to build the resources and services necessary for a teen mental health initiative, you must start from within the organization, which is why staff education and training are essential.

Supporting a Culture of Change

One way to find out what staff members know about mental disorders is for an in-service training. Depending on the size of your staff, the speaker may have to present several times at different locations. If possible, offer this presentation during a staff development day. Before booking the speaker, ask a staff member from your local public health department if he would be able to assist you. If not, contact your local NAMI chapter, or local mental health advocacy group, to see if a representative would be willing to talk about mental disorders with the staff. If you are still unable to book a speaker, reach out to the local mental health community to see if you can have licensed clinician discuss mental health. Keep in mind, by connecting with fellow city departments or nonprofits, you will have a better chance of booking a speaker free of charge.

Whatever you decide, training is important as the staff will gain a better understanding of why you and your teens want to launch a teen mental health initiative. Furthermore, by having this dialogue with the staff, you will get a consensus on how your work culture perceives mental disorders and provide evidence that, even in libraries, the library needs to do a better job about serving patrons with mental disorders. If you are unable to provide a speaker, invite staff members from every department to join a focus group. Here are some questions you can ask the focus group:

- Have you assisted a person with mental illness?
- Were you able to assist the patron confidently?
- Do you feel like you have the ability to assist a patron during a mental health crisis?
- Do you believe the library can better serve patrons with mental illness?
- If a patron asks for local mental health services, do you know where to direct him or her?

By speaking with representatives from all aspects of library service, you will get a better idea as to what front-line staff experiences versus the staff who works behind the scenes. Regardless of position, and responsibilities, mental health crisis occurs anywhere at any time, so it's important to know if everyone understands what mental disorders are and how to respond to those situations.

As you gather your feedback, take a good look at what the library currently offers for people with mental disorders. Also take a look at your policies and see if patrons with mental health challenges are afforded the same access to the library as other patrons. Here is one way you can adapt your behavior and lending policies to include teen with mental illness:

- Review the wording of your policies (i.e., is the policy easy to read, clear, and concise?
- Does the policy provide an explanation of enforcement process where teens can easily understand why they are being asked to leave?
- Are your current policies provide a certain level of tolerance for teens with mental illness?

By taking all of these steps, you should have the information you need to learn more about the staff and develop their skills when working with patrons with mental disorder. Why is this important? Just like with any other new service, if the staff knows what it is and is prepared to provide these services, the better the outcome for both patrons and the staff.

As you develop teen mental health services and resources, be sure that you inform the staff as soon as you can. Instead of notifying them at the last minute about new services and resource, it's best to give plenty of notice as they may need training to support new services. For example, if a teen is experiencing a mental health crisis and is asking for help, the staff should know whom to contact. Also, the staff needs to understand the difference between information seeking and an emergency so they will need to understand the signs of a mental health crisis. If these are the types of services that you would like to have at the library, it's important to provide the staff with training or, the very least, a script that helps the staff communicate with a patron during a mental health crisis. In order to provide this training, partnerships with your local public health department and mental health organizations can come in handy. If the staff is interested in teen cultural competency trainings, or youth mental health information sessions, working with these partners will help the library connect teens to these services.

Supporting Staff beyond Trainings

When introducing an initiative, realize that some of your coworkers may not embrace these new kinds of services, at least not immediately. While they may have their own personal reasons, it's worth noting that, traditionally, providing mental health resources and programs is outside of the library scope. When working with coworkers who truly believe that the library holds no responsibility for the medical needs of their patrons, gently remind them that we are not providing medical care—we are providing access to information and resources that patrons can use to get help. Libraries have always been a place for people to learn, so providing a class about mindfulness is the same as providing a storytime or genealogy lecture. Although this may not convince some of your coworkers, it's important that you encourage and support them through this process, especially if they encounter a teen experiencing a mental health crisis.

To prepare for the event a staff member encounters a teen with a mental disorder, provide them with a toolkit on how to have a positive interaction with the teen. By having this information handy, not only is the staff able to answer questions that patrons may have but they also know that they can contact you in case they have any questions.

When creating this toolkit, include the following topics:

- What to do during a crisis
- How to de-escalate a situation between patrons and teens

- Tips on how to serve teens with mental disorders
- Where to locate resources

Along with toolkits, provide the staff with an outline of teen mental health services and resources that includes the following:

- Mental health information the library provides
- List of mental health programs that the library offers
- Items in the collection that teens can check out

In addition to staff training, contact your local public health department to see if they would be willing to send over a social worker to visit the library in the event teens need assistance. While some libraries have started employing their own social workers, others simply don't have the funding. However, if the Public Health Department is willing to provide a social worker in the event of an emergency, that can be just as beneficial. Again, make it clear that library staff is not expected to diagnose and treat teens with mental disorders, but having that extra support would help the teens and staff immensely.

Creating a Safe Space

Now that the staff is more aware of teens' mental illness, it's time to think about the library environment that teens inhabit—and make sure they are safe for all teens. Libraries are public buildings where no one can be denied access as long as they are abiding by the policies set forth by the library. However, in order for libraries to become safe spaces, you need more than just a room designated for teens. You need an environment where all teens can feel accepted for who they are and where bullying and harassment are not tolerated.

Before dedicating your space as a safe space, it's important to check your behavior and collection policies to see if they are inclusive and provide rules in regard to harassment and intimidation. If your library's policies don't align with the purpose of your safe space, speak to your managers to see if amendments can be made. Understand that declaring a safe space just doesn't just happen overnight. It must be backed up by the right policies and enforcement. If you are trying to revise current policies, you will need to go through the proper channels to have them amended, so work closely with your management, be persistent, and follow up. Once these policies support the safe space, teens will be able to take refuge in your building with a guarantee that they will be able to rest and enjoy themselves free of discrimination or criticism.

GLSEN Teen Safe Space Kit

With policies in hand, the next step is to create the foundation for the safe space. The Gay Lesbian Straight Education Network (GLSEN) created a step-by-step toolkit for schools and libraries to create welcoming, supportive, and safe environments for LGBTQ students. By using the same principles that GLSEN outlines, a library can dedicate itself as a safe space for teens with mental disorders by

- Knowing how mental disorders affect teens
- Understanding how the library and community can support teens with mental disorders
- Educating the public about teen mental disorders
- Advocating for teens with mental disorders

In order to adhere to these principles, libraries must, first of all, make itself known as a harassment-free zone. After declaring your safe space, educate the public by providing handouts or pamphlets discussing mental disorders, why the library supports teens with mental disorders, and how the library will assist these teens. If you would like to order pamphlets that you can provide the public, contact the following organizations:

National Institute on Mental Health
https://www.nimh.nih.gov/health/publications/index.shtml
Office of Adolescent Health-Health & Human Services
https://www.hhs.gov/ash/oah/resources-and-
    training/adolescent-health-library/mental-health-resources-and-
    publications/index.html
Teen Line Store
https://teenlineonline.org/store/
Teen Mental Health Magazine Series
http://teenmentalhealth.org/product/teenmentalhealth-speaks-
    magazine/

If you have a public relations staff, work closely with them and your administration to put out announcements for the public. Also consider working with these colleagues to draft an outline of the safe space that includes the what, why, where, and when. By announcing this new service, your teen advisory board (TAB), or focus groups, can assist with the implementation and marketing of the safe space. By encouraging your TABs to be a part of this initiative, you will have support of a very influential group of young people who will be more than enthusiastic to tell their friends that your library cares about teens and they should use the library more often. To order, or download, the GLSEN Safe Space Toolkit, visit: https://www.glsen.org/safespace.

Safe Space Signage

As you work on creating a safe space and notifying the public, you need something that is going to grab attention. In other words, declare your safe space with clear and concise signage. Whether it's a poster, or an 8 ½ by 11-inch printouts, what matters is the words and the policies that back up those words. If your library's policies align with the purpose of your safe space, then make it known by using signs, but also educate your staff as to what a safe space is and what the rules are. Place additional signs explaining the rules of a safe space in the event a patron has questions or feel he or she is being harassed.

When it comes to creating signs, use words and phrases that are direct, but simple. Also, many organizations have created signs that are already in place, so don't feel like you have to reinvent the wheel. In fact, the Safe Schools Coalition, based out of Seattle, Washington, developed a simple sign based off of the Boulder County Health Department that uses the following wording to declare a safe space:

SAFE ZONE—This space RESPECTS all aspects of people including race, ethnicity, gender expression, sexual orientation, socio-economic background, age, religion, and ability. This SAFE ZONE poster was adapted from a Boulder County Health Department poster and is brought to you by your friends at the Safe Schools Coalition. To print more posters, please visit www.safeschoolscoalition.org.[1]

For more information about creating a safe space in your library:

Bell, Steven. "Make the Academic Library a Safe Space . . . Literally | From the Bell Tower." *Library Journal*. September 6, 2016. https://lj. libraryjournal.com/2016/09/opinion/steven-bell/make-the-acade mic-library-a-safe-spaceliterally-from-the-bell-tower/.

Cellucci, Anita. "The School Library as a Safe Space." What the Research Says: Reading Self-Selected Books for Fun | Edu@ scholastic. January 4, 2017. http://edublog.scholastic.com/ post/school-library-safe-space.

"Libraries as Safe Spaces." GLSEN. https://www.glsen.org/ article/libraries-safe-spaces.

Vaillancourt, Shawn. "Libraries as Safe Spaces." *American Libraries Magazine*. March 4, 2016. https://americanlibrariesmagazine.org/2012/12/11/libraries-as-safe-spaces

Winkelstein, Julie Ann. "Safe in the Stacks: Community Spaces for Homeless LGBTQ Youth." Advocacy, Legislation & Issues. February 20, 2018. http://www.ala.org/rt/glbtrt/tools/homeless-lgbtq-youth.

DE STIGMATIZE MENTAL ILLNESS THROUGH DIALOGUE AND COMMUNITY BUILDING

Another key element that will assist in building a library teen mental health initiative is to invite your community to join in a positive dialogue to de-stigmatize mental illness. Whether it's providing handouts explaining why the library supports this initiative or bringing in a speaker to talk about mental health, encourage your patrons to join the conversation. More importantly, invite your TAB and/or local teen youth groups and organizations to join in the conversation, because this initiative was meant to support teens with mental illness so their opinions are just as important.

Teen Mental Health Training Seminar

When the Pasadena Public Library TAB, in conjunction with library staff, sponsored a teen mental health training, 20 teens spent 2 hours with a licensed social worker from the Pasadena Public Health Department discussing mental illness. In this training, teens learned the signs of mental illness and, if they think a friend or a family member might have a mental illness, what they can do to get them help. This training allowed teens to ask the questions they needed answers for, and they appreciated the information that was presented before them.

Tap into Your Teen Advisory Boards

When it comes to mental health disorders, teens know a lot more than you might think. In fact, many will talk about their own struggles with anxiety or depression because they see it as a legitimate problem that they, and their peers, witness or experience on a regular basis. If you want to have a real and honest discussion about mental health and mental illness, there is no better place to start than with your TABs. Not only are they invested in the library; they have the potential to create change in their community. If the library has yet to establish a TAB, turn informal conversations into programs with an incentive to get them into the building (i.e., food, volunteer hours, or prizes of some sort). Or you could invite local youth organizations to come to the library and talk about mental health. By compiling the feedback from discussions, you not only accumulate the facts you need to develop a proposal to create mental health–related services and programs but also can build a core group of teens who can help you implement and promote these new ideas and services.

Before initiating a conversation about mental illness with teens, keep in mind that you should approach this topic in a way that will inspire them to want to be a part of developing new services and programs. The best way to get this conversation going is to ask your TAB to pinpoint areas of service that are great and those that are not so great. As the group discusses these topics, talk about how libraries can do more, such as providing teens with programs and resources that can help teens with specific needs.

> In 2016, my colleague and I sat down with our TAB to talk discuss the library's 2016 teen services strategic plan, which, in this case, focused on an underserved group of teens. The reason why we wanted to discuss underserved teens is because we realized that we needed to do more for those who could benefit the most from library services and incorporate the needs of teens into everything we do. Not only was this exciting for us, it gave us the opportunity to try something different that would require a significant amount of work from our TAB members and a lot of coordinating on our part.
>
> As we discussed what to focus on, we mentioned four groups of teens that could benefit from library services and resources that included: teens with disabilities, teens experiencing homelessness, teen parents, and teens with mental illness. The reason we selected these four groups were based on teen patrons who use the library, but for whom there aren't programs and services relevant to their specific needs. While explaining these underserved groups of teens, we made sure to explain to teens who they are and what they need from the library. In other words, do your homework by talking to parents, teens, caregivers, and advocates from the community. Use this information to not only connect with these partners but take this information to craft a proposal that will not only appeal to teens, but to meet the needs of these specific user groups.

By involving your TAB to be a part of this initiative, you not only have a dedicated set of teens who love using the library but also have a passionate group of teen librarians and advocates who can have a huge impact on how we deliver services and programs. We are living in exciting times because this generation of teens has an extraordinary capacity for compassion and empathy for one another, which is why we need to invite them to the table and help us connect with teens who don't realize that the library can do a lot more than provide free books and Internet—it can provide resources that can potentially save a life. When presenting to your management about the need for a teen mental health initiative, use as much of this feedback as you can as they provide evidence as why these services are needed and wanted. In fact, bring some of your TAB members to the meeting and give them a few moments to talk to your management about why they support this initiative and how it can help the library connect with teens in the community.

Connect with Local Youth Organizations

In the event you don't have a TAB, connect with local youth organizations. Whether it's a local student body from a nearby high school or an informal group of teens who use the library, their opinions can be helpful in building your teen mental health initiative. In fact, if you recruit a group of teens who hang out in the library, ask them to be a part of a special focus group. Creating this focus group will not only help these teens build leadership skills but also provide them a platform where they can voice their suggestions or concerns.

As you work with your teen focus group, teens will have a unique opportunity to not only learn about program planning but, by teaching them how to create, implement, and market this initiative, teens will see how a few ideas can transform into something real. By engaging and empowering teens to advocate for teens with mental illness, they are cultivating the necessary skills to become leaders while practicing empathy. While it's important to meet the needs of teens with mental illness, it's just as important that teens learn how to speak up for those who may not be able to. More importantly, teach teens that they have the power to advocate for teens in need.

Connecting Teens with Local Mental Health Organizations

As you work with teens, provide them with the information they need to understand mental disorders, which can be posted in a web guide on the library's website or documented in handouts published by the library. Through the partnerships you developed with public health and/or other mental health organizations, provide your TAB and/or focus groups with training and workshops. By asking your local mental health organizations to provide trainings, teens can ask questions, and even advice, from the experts. Also, by getting to know these organizations, teens can tell their friends and family about these resources that can be helpful in the case of an emergency.

When you ask teens to participate in this initiative, provide them with the same opportunities as the staff. Although teens are volunteering their time, they are just as important in promoting this initiative, so they should be just as prepared and informed as the staff. Also, by hosting these opportunities for teens, your partners will be able to witness the courage and dedication of the teens and demonstrate to the mental health community that teens are very aware of mental disorders and are interested in learning how to advocate for themselves and those who might not know how. Here are some YouTube videos worth watching as these teens proclaim to their audience, and the entire world, what it is like to live with a mental disorder and how they have turned their disorders into advocacy.

Moore, Ellie Marie. "Burnt Pages (Youth Mental Health Documentary)." YouTube. October 23, 2016. https://www.youtube.com/watch?v=xEjvol4k5OQ&list=PLe8Nu3lRhHqblhHGlnj0p3uNkRMiFq5ha.

Shinnick, Megan. "The Truth about Teen Depression | Megan Shinnick | TEDxYouth@BeaconStreet." YouTube. February 6, 2015. https://www.youtube.com/watch?v=txJGm6zhiBA.

Southworth, Amanda. "Tales from a Teenage Mental Health Advocate | Amanda Southworth | TEDxPasadena." YouTube. November 16, 2017. https://youtu.be/pLOagmZTWmM.

CONSTRUCTING A TEEN MENTAL HEALTH RESOURCE CENTER

Now it's time to assemble all the information. You may decide to use a simple display to a dedicated space/center, including flyers, pamphlets, materials in various formats, and computer access to resources. Depending on the amount of information you receive from partners, all of this needs to be placed strategically and be easily accessible. Whether it's in the teen center, along the wall next to your teen nonfiction stacks, or near the restrooms, it is imperative that this information is displayed in a conspicuous place that teens cannot avoid. Why? Teens struggling with mental disorders may feel scared or ashamed. By displaying this information in a place that is widely accessible, teens can pick up whatever they want, whenever they want without fearing anyone is looking at them.

In addition to making your partners' information visible, consider developing other information resources, like pathfinders and book lists, that discuss mental disorders. The Pasadena Public Library provides a bookmark that lists call numbers for tough topics as well as an online booklist that can be accessed at http://cityofpasadena.libguides.com/teenbooks/mentalhealth. By creating materials in house, you will be able to boost your reach with the teen community, and these guides will help you maintain and develop your collections even further. Moreover, by providing these materials and resources, you will be able to add another dimension to your initiative, which is to bring teens into the library to discover community resources.

As you build your teen mental health collection, consider expanding your nonfiction collection. While there are fiction titles that focus on various mental disorders, having a reasonable selection of nonfiction titles can supplement your fiction collection, as these titles can provide teens with medical information about symptoms and treatment options. Here are some great nonfiction titles that you might want to include in your teen collection:

Breel, Kevin. *Boy Meets Depression, Or, Life Sucks and Then You Die/Or, Life Sucks and Then You Live.* New York: Harmony Books, 2015.

Letran, Jacqui. *I Would, but My Damn Mind Won't Let Me!: A Teen's Guide to Controlling Their Thoughts and Feelings.* Asheville, NC: Healed Mind, 2016.

Palmer, Libbi. *The PTSD Workbook for Teens: Simple, Effective Skills for Healing Trauma.* Oakland, CA: New Harbinger, 2013.

Schab, Lisa M. *Beyond the Blues: A Workbook to Help Teens Overcome Depression.* Oakland, CA: Instant Help Books, 2008.

Schab, Lisa M. *The Anxiety Workbook for Teens: Activities to Help You Deal with Anxiety & Worry.* Oakland, CA: Instant Help Books, 2008.

Shannon, Jennifer, and Doug Shannon. *The Anxiety Survival Guide for Teens: CBT Skills to Overcome Fear, Worry & Panic.* Oakland, CA: Instant Help Books an Imprint of New Harbinger Publications, 2015.

Shapiro, Lawrence E. *Stopping the Pain: A Workbook for Teens Who Cut and Self-injure.* Oakland, CA: New Harbinger Publications, 2008.

Snyder, Kurt, Raquel E. Gurd, and Linda Wasmer Andrews. *Me, Myself, and Them: A Firsthand Account of One Teenager's Experience with Schizophrenia*. New York: Oxford University Press, 2007.

Toner, Jacqueline B., and Claire A. B. Freeland. *Depression: A Teen's Guide to Survive and Thrive*. Washington, DC: Magination Press, American Psychological Association, 2016.

As new titles become available, try to promote these titles to teens. If you have a website, blog, or libguide, make all of this information available online. As you add materials, make an attractive display that includes your pathfinders and handouts for teens to take. Along with adding book titles for teens, consider adding materials for parents as they may need information in case they suspect their teen might have a mental disorder. Here is a great list of books recommended to parents, educators, and mentors, you may want to include in your collection:

Jensen, Frances E. *The Teenage Brain: A Neuroscientist's Survival Guide to Raising Adolescents and Young Adults*. New York: Harper Paperbacks, 2016.

Josephs, Sheila Achar. *Helping Your Anxious Teen: Positive Parenting Strategies to Help Your Teen Beat Anxiety, Stress, and Worry*. Oakland, CA: New Harbinger Publications, 2016.

Mondimore, Francis Mark, and Patrick Kelly. *Adolescent Depression: A Guide for Parents*. Baltimore: Johns Hopkins University Press, 2015.

Perry, Bruce Duncan, and Maia Szalavitz. *The Boy Who Was Raised as a Dog: And Other Stories from a Child Psychiatrist's Notebook: What Traumatized Children Can Teach Us about Loss, Love, and Healing*. New York: Basic Books, 2017.

Steinberg, Laurence D. *You and Your Adolescent: The Essential Guide for Ages 10–25*. New York: Simon & Schuster, 2011.

Westreich, Laurence Michael. *A Parent's Guide to Teen Addiction: Professional Advice on Signs, Symptoms, What to Say, and How to Help*. New York: Skyhorse Publishing, 2017.

White, Aaron M., and Scott Swartzwelder. *What Are They Thinking?!: The Straight Facts about the Risk-Taking, Social-Networking, Still-Developing Teen Brain*. New York: W.W. Norton & Company, 2013.

After creating a resource/information center, be sure to advertise it. One way to market your center is to ask your teens to publicize it. When you meet for your monthly meeting, give your teens pointers on how to present your initiative. Invite teens to important meetings and give them a few minutes to discuss what the initiative is and why it's important for teens. Also, host an unveiling event where you invite the community to learn about the center and how the teen initiative can help those in need. As you plan your event, use all your publicity outlets and invite local media (if possible) to interview teens, staff, and partners. Share your pamphlets, pathfinders, and/or flyers with community partners as they may be able to put your information in their offices or waiting rooms. Teens need all the support they can get during these difficult times, which is why they should know that the library is there to help them as well.

NOTE

1. "Posters, Stickers, Cards—Safe Schools Coalition." Safe Schools Coalition. http://www.safeschoolscoalition.org/RG-posters.html.

6

◇ ◇ ◇

BUILDING AND PROMOTING
BETTER SERVICES FOR TEENS

As you work with teens to build a safe space, a mental health resource center, and a collection that will support teens with mental disorders, think about other service aspects that teens can assist with. Whether it's about adapting current programming, changing marketing strategies, or creating new programs, teens can provide a unique perspective on what the library can do to enhance current programs and services. Also, consult with teens in regard to evaluating current services, and don't take anything personally if they don't like what is currently being offered. In fact, be open minded to teens' ideas as they are dedicated to making the library a better place for all teens. As you review any ideas that teens may have already suggested, organize them based on what resources you have available and, depending on their popularity, implement them based on need. Lastly, when working with teens to enhance, or create, new services, include reaching out to the entire community as they may be to help you develop your teen mental health initiative.

BUILDING PARTNERSHIPS WITH YOUTH AND MENTAL HEALTH ORGANIZATIONS

While it is important to have the support of your own library and mental health community for your initiative, it is just as important to connect with youth organizations in your city or county, such as the following:

- Boys & Girls Scouts of America
- Key Club
- Amnesty International
- Boys and Girls of America
- Student councils
- LGBTQ/Straight Alliances
- Local honor societies
- Local high school faith-based groups
- Youth cultural clubs
- Youth groups for teens experiencing homelessness
- Youth foster groups

If you have yet to reach out to youth organizations, connect with these groups and ask them to be a part of your initiative. Through these partnerships, the library can inspire other organizations to support the library's teen mental health initiative and the library can then connect these youth groups to local mental health resources as well. Whether it's through a joint meeting or just passing information to each group, teens need to know these organizations exist in the event they experience signs of a mental disorder or know someone who is.

By promoting your initiative to teens who may not have access to traditional health care services, your library will also serve as a resource hub—a place where health care providers can leave their contact information and/or list of services that teens can contact. Furthermore, if you notice a significant need for mental health resources, invite some of your partners to stop by the library and meet with teens who need help. If this is not an option, contact the social workers that work with your city and ask them for their contact information in the event of a teen needs help in getting access to care.

While it's good to have a resource on hand that is willing and able to help out in a crisis situation, there may be a time where your primary contact is not available. If this happens, reassure the teen that this person can help them and, if possible, ask them to leave their contact information for you to relay to the social worker. If that is not an option, ask the teen to return on another day when you know your contact will be available.

Whatever you do, do not give up. Depending on the teen's situation, and if they are in danger, trust your instincts and call the paramedics as soon as possible. If it turns out that a teen isn't in imminent danger, it is better to be safe than sorry. If a teen gets mad at you for alerting emergency services, explain to him or her that it is in the teen's best interest to get help as you are worried about him or her.

The more aware teens become of the library as a resource to help them advocate for their own mental health, the more informed they will be in general. Also, let your partners know that in addition to information, the library provides a safe space for teens, and inform them of any related programs. As you have these conversations with youth groups, introduce them to the teens who are helping you with the initiative. Not only is this a great experience for teens but also help teens build compassion and empathy while empowering others to take control of their mental health. By working with local youth groups, a lot of amazing things can happen. More importantly, as you grow these relationships, always evaluate and check in with them as you want to ensure that the library is meeting the needs of the organization and vice versa.

DEVELOPING TEEN ADVOCACY PROGRAMS

In order to teach teens the importance of advocacy, you need to provide them with the knowledge and the tools to do so. As a teen librarian, you are an advocate who works to ensure that teens meet their potential, which is why you plan programs and services to help them achieve academic and personal success. For teens experiencing mental disorders, their greatest advocates are their parents and/or caregivers. However, if parents and/or caregivers are absent, abusive, or teens feel like they can't disclose their disorder to their parents because of cultural or religious reasons, teens will need to learn how to help themselves. As part of your initiative, consider providing programs or workshops that teach teens how to seek out help. Furthermore, provide opportunities for teens to learn how to talk with their peers, or family members, about mental disorders and where to seek help. Here are some ideas on how to start these conversations.

Teen Mental Health Advocacy Seminars

One of the best resources you can rely is your local NAMI chapter. Known as one of the biggest grassroots advocacy groups, NAMI can provide teens with the tools they need to help them advocate for their own health, and it is accessible 24/7. If you are able to connect with your local chapter, ask if one of their representatives would be willing to come into the library and talk about mental health advocacy with TAB and teen patrons. NAMI also provides families and parents with free informational workshops so you could do a series of advocacy workshops for teens and their families.

Another great resource you can contact to provide advocacy programs is your city and county mental health advocacy groups. While NAMI is one of the better-known advocacy groups, don't forget to look within your own city, as these organizations would be more than happy to work with the library.

By offering teens the opportunity to learn how to help for themselves and for others, the library will help teens build valuable life skills in the future. And this is where your partners from local youth groups and mental health organizations can assist you. For example, invite a mental health organization to provide teens with workshops about suicide prevention or signs of mental disorders. Or youth leadership groups can help teens build interpersonal skills. Ask your public health department to provide a program on how teens can get confidential mental health services. By helping teens better understand mental disorders, and giving them the opportunity to learn advocacy, teens will benefit greatly, learning how to help others or themselves.

ADAPTING TRADITIONAL PROGRAMS

One way to provide programming that includes teen mental disorders is to adapt the programs you already have. In fact, you may already offer programs that can be used to help teens learn coping skills through art and physical fitness programs. Also, programs such as teen book clubs can help teens learn about mental illness as they read and discuss the character's battle with mental illness. All of these traditional programs can be a gateway to even bigger conversations about mental illness and this is how you can guide that discussion.

Teen Book Clubs

If your library provides a monthly teen book club, help kick off your mental health initiative discussing mental disorders with your teen book club. Given the wealth of titles that discuss everything from bullying, abuse, and suicide, create a list of what your library has on hand and work with your teen advisory boards. This doesn't mean that your book club would focus exclusively on mental health issues. Obviously, you don't want to overwhelm your readers or force books on them that they won't enjoy.

If you do this, keep in mind that it is highly unlikely that all of your teens will recognize if a character is experiencing a mental disorder, so there is no need to change your discussion format to accommodate a discussion on mental disorders. If you feel uncomfortable discussing the science behind mental disorders, invite a representative from one of your partner institutions to the discussion. That way, if your teens have questions about mental disorders, you have an expert to answer their questions. Teens can use this information to discuss what's going on in the book especially if you see that any of the participants become uncomfortable.

Book to Movie Discussions

Another program that works well for mental health discussions is one where the participants read a book and watch the movie adaptation. Hollywood tends to interpret books and mental illness in a skewed way, which could generate a lot of interesting conversation. For example, the movie based on the late Ned Vizzini's *It's Kind of a Funny Story* is a great example of a book about a teen named Craig, who is feeling depressed and checks himself into his local hospital. While the movie does a fairly decent job of telling the story, teens will also learn how books are not easily translated to film. One thing you may want to mention to teens is that film directors often base their films on certain aspects of the book. While this may be necessary for the film, ask teens to be open minded as they watch the movie. As you and the teens write discussion questions, keep these inconsistencies in mind as they may add to the discussion. For example, does the movie portray mental illness the way the author does? If not, what could have the directors done differently to portray mental illness?

Again, you may wish to invite a partner or mental health expert to your discussion, so when teens discuss the inconsistencies between the book and movie versions, they can explain technical points. For example, they might want to explain why Craig feels the way he does and how his talent for art can help him cope with his stress. By having an expert present, teens can ask all kinds of questions and get answers. Also, your expert can introduce his or her organization to teens and talk about what they do and how they can help teens like Craig. Be sure to ask your expert to bring pertinent flyers or pamphlets to add to the mental health resource center and to hand out at your discussion.

Teens always learn something valuable at these discussions. While the point of the program is to discuss the differences and similarities between a book and its movie adaption, having an expert can shed light on the issues that the characters in the book are experiencing. Even if the book is fiction, the situations may be very real. And by participating in the discussion, your expert may learn more about young-adult literature and about how teens perceive mental disorders. Lastly, introducing teens to mental health experts in the context of a book discussion is a great way for them to connect in a nonthreatening situation. So, if and when they do need help, making contact won't be as difficult. For book and movie recommendations, turn to Appendix A.

Arts and Crafts Programs

According to the American Art Therapy Association, "Art therapy is used to improve cognitive and sensorimotor functions, foster self-esteem and self-awareness, cultivate emotional resilience, promote insight, enhance social skills, reduce and resolve conflicts and distress, and advance societal and ecological change."[1] Based on this definition, art therapy is not just for people with mental disorders; it's for everyone who needs to express themselves and has the ability to heal and empower. In fact, Maheshwari, Ordner, Agarwal, and Retamero (2014) noted that "[i]ndividuals with mental illnesses may not always be verbally expressive; however, they may display emotions through creative expressions such as music, poetry, or art. The use of art also helps them reflect on their thoughts, desires, and challenges."[2] Here is a list of arts and crafts programs that allow teens to express themselves:

- Sewing projects
- Acrylic or watercolor painting series
- Manga or comic workshops
- Mixed media art projects
- Origami workshops
- Jewelry-making workshops
- Knitting and/or crocheting workshops

As you plan arts and craft programs, contact a local therapist to help you create a program that incorporates elements of art therapy to help teens channel their emotions. If possible, invite him or her to come to the workshops to discuss the process and reasoning behind the project. To learn more about art therapy, the American Therapy Association, check out their website at: https://arttherapy.org/. To find art therapists in your community, the best place to start is to contact your partners or your public health department.

Life Skills Programs

While arts and crafts programs can help teens manage their emotions and fears, life skills programs can be just as effective in teaching them how to better communicate, handle stress, and manage their emotions. One program that can assist teens in documenting their feelings that can be incorporated into daily routines is journaling. Journaling can be done on a daily or routine basis and can help teens process their feelings in a safe space and in a healthy way. Journaling allows teens to express their feelings without the risks of being judged or misunderstood.

Invite a mental health expert or partner to discuss the therapeutic effects of journaling. According to Harvard Medical School (2016), "The act of thinking about an experience, as well as expressing emotions, seems to be important. In this way, writing helps people to organize thoughts and give meaning to a traumatic experience."[3] By hosting this event, teens can discover the power of self-expression and incorporate it into their daily routines to help them cope with stress. If teens have any questions, or want to learn more about journaling, experts can assist them. Make this event hands on where teens decorate their own journal. As teens decorate, ask the expert to provide a couple of sample journal topics that teens can write about if they are feeling stressed, anxious, or depressed. If teens seem more interested in the decorating process, it's okay because at least they are learning that they can put their journals into good use.

Another type of program that has risen in popularity, in regard to managing mental disorders, is a program that focuses on mindfulness. Mindfulness is the practice of being completely aware of where you are no matter what is going on around you. In other words, it's the ability to come back to your center even when you feel like things are out of whack. For teens with mental disorders, mindfulness can be a great coping skill as it employs the art of meditation to bring teens back to their center. According to the American Psychiatric Association (2016), "A great deal of research has documented physical health benefits of mindfulness, such as an improved immune system, lower blood pressure, and better sleep. Mindfulness has also been linked to mental health benefits, such as reduced stress and anxiety, and improved concentration and focus, less emotional reactivity."[4]

Mindfulness is another life skill that can help teens manage their emotions. In fact, schools like Robert W. Coleman Elementary School, in Baltimore, Maryland, are replacing their detention programs with mindfulness. CNN (2016) reported that "kids are instead referred to the Mindful Moment Room, an oasis of colorful tapestries and beanbag chairs, oil diffusers and herbal tea, where they practice deep-breathing exercises, meditate and talk."[5] By employing mindfulness techniques, teens have the opportunity to learn how to recognize their anger, process it, and then return to neutral. In other words, teens are developing coping skills, which they can carry on well into adulthood.

Draw upon your community partners and local mediation centers when planning mindfulness programs. While mindfulness is gaining traction in regard to mental health management, resources may not be easily accessible, which is where your partners can help connect you to the right professionals. With this type of workshop, try offering a series where teens can practice with an instructor and ask them questions if needed. Depending on what meditation techniques the instructor employs, teens may not be required to submit a liability waiver if your city, or county, doesn't have liability insurance. The best aspect about mindfulness is that there isn't a whole lot to set up other than an enclosed room with privacy. While aromatherapy and pillows can make teens more comfortable, they are not mandatory. In fact, ask teens if they think these items would support their practice; otherwise, keep it simple.

Physical Fitness Programs

Another sure-fire way for teens to channel their negative thoughts and stress is to engage them in activities that are good for the body as well. One program that the library can host is a teen yoga workshop. Although reasons vary as to why certain individuals practice yoga, one reason why you should introduce the practice is that it provides relief for those experiencing anxiety and depression. Harvard Medical School (2009) notes that "yoga functions like other self-soothing techniques, such as meditation, relaxation, exercise, or even socializing with friends [and] for many patients dealing with depression, anxiety, or stress, yoga may be a very appealing way to better manage symptoms."[6]

Yoga is comprised of movements and breathing techniques to help people strengthen their bodies and their well-being. As in meditation, those who practice yoga use their breath to move their energy, which brings oxygen to the brain and body. From a physiological stand point, breathing in oxygen, combined with movement, provides the brain and the body with much-needed energy without having to run five miles and provides relief. This program can help teens channel their feelings by taking care of their minds and bodies.

If your library already offers programs like yoga, sponsor an event just for teens, so they can learn and practice the fundamentals. The first thing you need to consider, prior to planning, is to check with your risk management department to see if you need to provide liability waivers. If waivers are not necessary, it's good to start with a very basic program that focuses on breathing and easy poses. If you decide to offer a program, ask your Teen Advisory Board (TAB) if they would be willing to help you with the marketing and participating in event. As for program supplies, consider purchasing basic mats, as not every teen has a mat of his or her own. Host the program in a location where teens can relax and move without fearing judgment or interruption. As for finding an instructor, ask your fellow staff members if they are veteran yoga practitioners or reach out to your community. If your budget is limited, or you can't find an instructor, you can always pop in a DVD from your collection. While this program is meant for teens, your participation will be just as beneficial, as teens will follow your lead.

SERVICES AND PROGRAMS FOR TEENS WITH MENTAL ILLNESS

As you adapt and create programs to help teens understand mental illness, consider implementing programs and services that benefit teens who are experiencing mental illness. To find out what services and programs will meet the needs of teens experiencing mental illness, solicit recommendations from teens or reach out to your mental health partners to see how the library can assist teens. Also, as you gather feedback, you will need to research the feasibility of some of these suggestions as libraries are slowly starting to provide in-house mental health services. Once you have gathered your information, including patron and partner feedback, sit down with your supervisor and discuss these ideas.

Teen Counseling Services in the Library

One thing to keep in mind about providing mental health services in the library is what is the scope of the service and how it will benefit teens and the library. For example, if teens recommend counseling services, there are several things to consider, such as the following:

- What organization(s) will provide the service (i.e., social worker, clinician, medical expert)?

- Where will the service take place (i.e., study room, meeting room, teen center)?
- How often and how long will the service be provided?
- Will registration be required or will it be a first-come-first service?
- Will these services be referral services or actual therapeutic services?
- What are the potential liabilities of offering the service (i.e., protecting confidentiality, parent notification, and/or HIPPA regulations)?
- Will these services be written into library policies?

These are just a few questions that may arise in your conversations about mental health services in the library. While it may seem daunting, it is worth discussing with supervisor and upper management, especially if your library is in an area where mental health services may not be widely available or the community you serve may not fully understand the impact of mental illness. If you feel resistance to the ideas, provide options or alternatives where the goal of the program is to ultimately connect teens with mental health care, which is where your community partners can help.

If any of your partners currently offer free counseling services, see if they would be willing to bring those services into the library. Since these services are already dedicated to providing mental health education and services for youth, the library can provide your partner with a meeting space where teens can access when necessary. If your library already offers meeting spaces for other free local services, such as business or legal clinics, be sure your local mental health partners have the same opportunity, especially if you see a need in the community. An example of this can found at the Eugene Public Library, located in Eugene, Oregon, which received a grant to partner with the White Bird Clinic to provide free, confidential, counseling services at the library.

To read more about the partnership of the Eugene Public Library and White Bird Clinic:

Staff, News. "Eugene Public Library Partners with White Bird Clinic to Offer Mental Health Counseling." *KMTR*, NBC, 18 March 2018, nbc16.com/news/local/eugene-public-library-partners-with-white-bird-clinic-to-offer-mental-health-counseling.

Instant Access to Mental Health Services

In the event that holding counseling services in the library is not available, you can provide teens access to local and national mental health services using resources you do have. If you have access to laptops for checkout, and you encounter a teen in distress, let teens use the laptop to connect with online mental health crisis chat or discussion boards. Another option is to inquire with your library administration to have a separate phone line in the teen area in case a teen needs to immediately connect with a crisis line. If you are able to get access to the phone line, see if you can get a cordless phone in the event it can be taken to a secluded spot. Here are some resources to create a handout or post on your library website for easy access:

National Child Abuse Hotline

Phone: 1–800–4-A-Child or 1-800-422-4453
Website: http://www.childhelp.org/hotline/
Sponsored by ChildHelp

National Domestic Violence Hotline

Phone: 1-800-799-7233
Phone (TTY): 1-800-787-3224
Website: http://www.thehotline.org/
Sponsored by the National Domestic Violence Hotline

National Helpline for Substance Abuse

Phone: 1–800–662-HELP
https://www.samhsa.gov/find-help/national-helpline
Sponsored by the Substance Abuse and Mental Health Services
    Association (SAMHSA)

National Runaway Safeline

Phone: 1-800-786-2929
Website: https://www.1800runaway.org
Sponsored by the National Runaway Safeline

National Sexual Assault Telephone Hotline

Phone: 800.656.HOPE (4673)
Chat: https://hotline.rainn.org/online/terms-of-service.jsp
Website: https://www.rainn.org/about-national-sexual-assault-
    telephone-hotline
Sponsored by Rape, Abuse, & Incest National Network (RAINN)

National Suicide Prevention Lifeline

Phone: 1-800-273-8255

Phone (for hearing impaired): 1-800-799-4889

Website: https://suicidepreventionlifeline.org/

Sponsored by the National Suicide Prevention Hotline

The Helpline

Phone: (800) 931–2237

Website: https://www.nationaleatingdisorders.org

Sponsored by the National Eating Disorder Association (NEDA

The Trevor Project

Phone: 866–488–7386

Text: "Trevor" to 1-202-304-1200

Website: https://www.thetrevorproject.org

Sponsored by the Trevor Project

Sharing Online Resources with Teens with Mental Illness

Along with providing access to mental health services, think about providing virtual programs that address the needs of teen with mental illness. What do these programs look like? These programs can be videos, podcasts, discussion boards, or even a web collection of resources that provides teens with information about mental illness. While it's always good to offer in-person workshops where teens can speak face-to-face with a mental health professional, consider offering an alternative that will help direct teens to care under the guise of anonymity. Grappling with a mental disorder can be incredibly frightening, confusing, and even shaming for teens, and these kinds of resources can help a teen learn more about their disorder and who to contact for help. Here are some great online resources to share with teens who want to better understand their disorder and they are not alone:

Discussion Boards:

Teen Help

http://www.teenhelp.org/forums/

Teen Line

https://teenlineonline.org/board/

Teen Tribe

https://support.therapytribe.com/teen-support-group/

Podcasts:

Mental Music
https://www.mentalmusic.org
This is Normal: A podcast about youth mental health
Download from Apple iTunes

Videos & Series:

BBC Three: Diaries of a Broken Mind
https://youtu.be/ATTbHvI-pVU
Mental Health: In Our Own Words:
https://www.youtube.com/watch?v=_y97VF5UJcc
Teen Connection
https://www.pbs.org/show/teen-connection/
When the Mask Comes Off: A Youth Perspective on Mental Illness
https://vimeo.com/94434796

This is just a sampling of what is available for teens with mental disorders. Take time to develop a list of online resources that teens have access to 24-7. As mentioned before, develop a list of online resources that you can post on your library website that you can direct teens to. Also, if there are computers designated for teens only, or lend laptops, work with your IT department to develop a list of mental health favorites on the Internet browsers installed on your computers. Just don't forget to also create print resources that can be accessed in your teen's areas, and be sure to keep some at the reference desk for colleagues to access.

ADVOCATING FOR TEENS THROUGH OUTREACH

By working with your mental health community, the library conveys to the teen community that it cares about their health and well-being. Furthermore, you are connecting your partners to parts of the community they may not have been able to reach before. With these relationships in place, you need to let the community know about your efforts through outreach. While outreach is standard practice for most library systems, for your initiative to success, you will need to expand its reach beyond the traditional back to school nights and class visits.

Outreach Events

As you put the final touches on your collections, programs, and services, think about the various events in your community that can help you promote the library's teen mental health initiative. While it's important to continue reaching out to schools, it's just as important to reach out to the rest of the community, especially youth organizations. As you reach out to local youth organizations, ask your mental health partners about the various outreaches they participate in to promote their services. For example, do these organizations participate in health fairs or expos? Ask if it would be possible for the library to participate in these events. If they have a youth connection, let youth organizations know that the library will be in attendance and you would like them to join your efforts. Although libraries are not traditionally known to participate in health-related events, we do provide access to health information. With the teen mental health initiative, the library is embarking on a journey that will take it into parts of the community that may not be aware that the library offers programs and resources to help teens with mental illness. Furthermore, with this initiative, inform the community that if it needs information on how to manage their disorders, the library provides free access to materials without judgment.

Mental Health Workshops for Parents and Mentors

With the teen mental health initiative, one major outcome you want to achieve is to teach teens how to advocate for themselves, in regard to their mental health. However, in order to reach that goal, it is just as important to invite adults—parents, guardians, older family members—to join the conversation. If a teen is experiencing a mental disorder, the best advocate they have is usually their parents, family, and friends. As part of your teen mental health initiative, include a component that empowers parents to take an active role in their teen's mental health. Whether it is through pamphlets, programs, or a resource guide full of information, let parents and other adults know that the library will continue to support them.

As you plan these workshops, think about the topics your partners can provide and how you can best utilize them. It's always a good idea to provide an overview of teen mental illness and what is being done to support teens. Once the community has an idea of what mental illness is, consider providing additional programs that address specific disorders based on the recommendations made by your youth groups. Also, if you work with advocacy groups, ask them to present or help you launch these programs as their resources can help you promote the library's services. By inviting the entire community to join the conversation, not only can the library promote healing within the community; it can join the ranks of other organizations that have taken the initiative to provide programs and services for teens.

The Children's Health Council Teen Mental Health Initiative

In 2016, the Children's Health Council (CHC), located in Palo Alto, California, launched its own teen mental health initiative, focusing on community engagement, mental health, education, and providing free, or low cost, mental health services to teens and their families. CHS also partnered with Stanford University to "engage partners to leverage complimentary resources and create a web of support that accurately and adequately captures the needs of teen mental health in the community."[7] Within a year, CHC has reported great success with 85 percent family satisfaction rate with clinical services and 90 percent rate of parents recommending their programs to other parents.

Another group of adults you will want to include in this component is youth mentors. Unfortunately, not every teen has a supportive grown-up in his or her life. However, mentoring programs such as Big Brother and Sisters of America can help fill the gap. If your community is home to youth-mentoring programs, get in touch with these organizations and let them know that the library is providing teen mental health resources, programs, and services. Above all, let them know that the library would welcome the groups to attend any workshops the library may be hosting as they could benefit from these trainings and discussions. Remember to provide these organizations with library materials and offer them the opportunity to meet with their mentees in the library.

By engaging and supporting parents and mentors, the library can increase teen mental health awareness within the community. If adults suspect that their teens may have a mental disorder, or just want to learn more about mental disorders, the library can provide them with a place, and resources, to get the information they need to assist their teens. Parents and mentors can be the greatest support system a teen has. Again, the more aware adults are of teen mental illness, the more confident and comfortable they are in discussing mental illness with their teens. Furthermore, by informing adults that the library has information available to help their teens, not only is this a step in the right direction, but it provides a sign of hope for adults who live, or work, with teens.

Lastly, continue inviting your community partners to help teens, parents, and mentors understand mental illness through programming.

Whether it's a conversation with mental health professionals or interactive workshops, it's important to reach out to the community. Unfortunately, the stigma surrounding mental illness can prevent people from getting treatment. Also, depending on the demographics of your community, mental health can be a taboo topic or just not discussed at all.

Media and Social Media Campaigns

Another effective way to promote the library's services and resources is to launch a media campaign. If the library is partnered with advocacy groups, work with them to promote the library and their services. Also, work with your communications departments to draft press releases that can be sent to the local newspapers and media. Along with traditional media outlets, launch a social media campaign simultaneously by working with local and state mental health advocacy groups to help spread the word. If your library has yet to engage in social media, now is the time, as millions of people, including teens, subscribe to these services. Furthermore, by working side by side with partners, you can connect with users who use library services or are not aware that the library is providing these kinds of resources.

Here is a list of mental health social media campaigns that can help you develop your own social media campaign:

- Each Mind Matters—https://www.eachmindmatters.org/
- #HereforYou—https://instagram-together.com/
- Be Vocal: Speak Up for Mental Health—http://www.bevocalspeak up.com/
- Time to Change: Let's End Mental Health Discrimination—https://www.time-to-change.org.uk/sites/default/files/In-Your-Corner-Campaign-Narrative.pdf
- See Me: The Power of Okay—https://www.seemescotland.org/our-movement-for-change/power-of-okay/

Empowering Teen Advocates

If you have invited your TAB or local youth organizations to help build and promote this initiative, it is vital to keep them engaged and active in the process. While input is important to the formation and implementation of the initiative, ask your teen advocates to assist with other projects, such as revising library policies. By inviting teens to join in the review process, you offer them the opportunity to learn what policies exist and why it is important that libraries adhere to these policies. As they learn the rhyme and reason behind policies, they will also learn how these policies are crafted and approved. This activity may not be interesting to some, but others will thrive on it. Inform teens that they are learning skills that can result in real change and can use throughout their lives. For teens who are truly passionate about this initiative, this opportunity can have a huge effect on them as they can take ownership of the end product, which is to make the library a safer and more welcoming place for teens with mental illness.

Another aspect of your initiative that teens can assist with is staff training. As a teen librarian, you know how to communicate honestly and openly with teens. However, staff in other departments may not be as knowledgeable, so ask teens to lead a conversation about communicating effectively with teens. This presentation can take form as a formal panel discussion or a simple Q&A forum, where the staff can honestly ask teens how adults should talk to teens in a productive manner. If presentations are not an option, ask your TAB or youth organizations to create a training video, where they can talk about how adults can approach teens, especially when they are in a vulnerable state. If you choose this route, ask teens to take the helm in how they want to present this video. While it may take some work, and organizing, on your part, this project can teach teens about the value of collaboration to educate and assist adults on how to really talk to teens. If this still isn't an option, ask teens to come up with an FAQ list of topics that adults may have when communicating with teens. Again, if you are asking the staff to fully support this initiative, you need to make sure that the staff has the tools they need to assist teens who need help. By asking TAB to assist in helping staff members better understand teens with mental illness, the staff needs to be comfortable with communicating with teens in general. Not only is this a great opportunity for the staff to learn more about teens; it conveys to teens that they are respected and supported by the entire library staff.

With teen advocates assisting with these kinds of projects, the one group who benefits the most from this collaboration is teens with mental illness. With teen advocates participating in the process of change, their passion and their dedication will have a profound effect on the library's teen mental health initiative. Teens can use these achievements and the accolades they receive to show their peers that the library truly cares about teens. Furthermore, by involving teens to participate in this initiative, you are helping them build emotional intelligence, which is not only vital in their development but necessary to create leaders of change. While teens with mental illness benefit the most from this initiative, the entire community will be affected in a positive way, which may inspire and lead other organizations to start their own youth initiatives.

NOTES

1. "About Art Therapy." https://arttherapy.org/about-art-therapy/.
2. "Writing about Emotions May Ease Stress and Trauma—Harvard Health." Harvard Health Blog. 2016. https://www.health.harvard.edu/healthbeat/writing-about-emotions-may-ease-stress-and-trauma.
3. Maheshwari, Subani, Ashley Ordner, Vishesh Agarwal, and Carolina Retamero. "Art Therapy in a Patient with Bipolar Disorder: Pictures Speak More Than a Thousand Words." *Psychiatric Times.* November 25, 2014. http://www.psychiatrictimes.com/bipolar-disorder/art-therapy-patient-bipolar-disorder-pictures-speak-more-thousand-words.
4. Haupt, Angela. "Mindfulness in Schools: When Meditation Replaces Detention." *U.S. News & World Report.* December 8, 2016. https://health.usnews.com/wellness/mind/articles/2016-12-08/mindfulness-in-schools-when-meditation-replaces-detention.
5. APA Staff. "Mindfulness Practices May Help Treat Many Mental Health Conditions." June 1, 2016. https://www.psychiatry.org/news-room/apa-blogs/apa-blog/2016/06/mindfulness-practices-may-help-treat-many-mental-health-conditions.
6. Harvard Health Publishing. "Yoga for Anxiety and Depression—Harvard Health." Harvard Health Blog. April 2009. https://www.health.harvard.edu/mind-and-mood/yoga-for-anxiety-and-depression.
7. Randolph, Michaela, and Yvonne Walters. "CHC Launches Mental Health Initiative for Teens—Expands Affordable Teen Therapy, Community Education and Engagement—Children's Health Council." Children's Health Council Resource Library. July 29, 2016. https://www.chconline.org/chc-launches-mental-health-initiative-teens-expands-affordable-teen-therapy-community-education-engagement/.

7
◇ ◇ ◇

PLANNING FOR THE FUTURE

Now that you have the knowledge to build and implement a teen mental health initiative, the next step is to figure out how you and your partners will track and evaluate the progress of your initiative. By tracking your progress, you will be able to document with notes and suggestions to streamline the planning process for the next phase of this initiative. Furthermore, getting this feedback from stakeholders can help you pinpoint what the community is looking for and what kind of community organizations will be able to assist in the implementation.

While there is no universal template for tracking and evaluating the progress of the teen mental health initiative, it is important to create a system that gathers the specific information you and your library needs. In other words, you and your partners will need to figure out what the objective of the initiative is and what types of data you should collect. If you currently employ an evaluation system, take a look at it and see if you need to expand upon it. Depending on the size of your initiative, and the types of programs and resources you offer, you may need to adapt your evaluation system to get the data you need. However, if you don't have a formal evaluation system in place, now is the time to work your partners to develop a system.

DEVELOPING AN EVALUATION SYSTEM

When developing your evaluation system, here are some areas to consider:

- Partnerships developed
- Outreaches conducted
- Number of hours TAB teens worked on the initiative
- Number of hours for staff training
- Number of programs implemented
- Attendance numbers
- Costs related to the programs
- Number of hours working with mental health community
- Feedback from the community about the teen mental health initiative

While this may seem like a long list, these elements can help you determine what aspects of the initiative work for the community, what aspects don't work, and how you might target specific needs. For example, does a presentation on coping skills have a bigger impact on teens than an interactive workshop, such as art therapy or yoga? By using data such as attendance numbers, patron feedback, and speaker feedback, you can find out what teens are most interested in and whether they learn something valuable. Furthermore, by tracking other aspects such as staff time spent on working with partners, outreach, and interacting with the public, you will get another set of data that will help you sustain partner relations.

DOCUMENTING AND EVALUATING THE TEEN MENTAL HEALTH INITIATIVE

Tracking Time and Staying Organized

The first step in developing a large-scale project like a teen mental health initiative is to keep track of the hours spent on the initiative—both your own and any other staff hours. Whether it's attending meetings, working with teens, meeting with partners, or working on your off-desk time, these hours spent are worth noting. By documenting your time, you will have a definitive number of hours you can use to help with future endeavors and assist colleagues who may be interested in launching their own teen mental health initiative. In fact, if you think you might apply for grant funding, keeping track of hours spent on projects is part of the reporting process, so make this a habit. Also, by having this documentation, you can create reports to share with staff, management, and/or library board. Along with hours, be sure to keep detailed notes of your meetings as you may want to record ideas that can be used for the future. Hold on to this information as it will be helpful in developing a master plan on how the library will continue to support the initiative.

While it's okay to file away your notes or keep them in the back of your mind, it is also helpful to review your notes periodically to see if you can add to them. By staying organized, you will be able to pull all of your ideas together, which will help you prepare for the next phase of the initiative. Lastly, share your notes with colleagues and partners by making them accessible through file-sharing resources like Dropbox or Google Docs or at least present them at your next meeting. By making this information available, you and your colleagues can refer to them as you start working on year two (or beyond) of your teen mental health initiative.

Program Evaluations

Program evaluations may already be a standard practice for you, but a teen mental health initiative is no exception. It is important that you provide evaluations for each event related to your initiative. If you have yet to use evaluation forms or don't have an official form to hand out, there are samples in Appendix B that you can customize. These forms don't have to fancy, but they should include important information that will assist you in the master-planning process. By using these forms, you can document what you could improve or enhance and if you want to host the same program in the future. Also, these forms can help you decide if you believe a program is worth developing depending on certain factors such as (a) attendance, (b) cost, and (c) future sustainability.

If you choose to create your own program evaluations, be sure to include the following:

- Name of event
- Brief description
- Presenter name
- Presenter organization
- Presenter contact information
- Patron feedback
- Presenter feedback
- Staff feedback
- Notes on how to improve or enhance
- Repeat program

While most program evaluations don't include a question about repeating a program, this information can be useful in deciding whether or not you want to offer the program more than once a year. For example, if you host a series of four stress release classes, and it's a massive success, it might be worth repeating. Of course, factors like cost and availability might determine whether and when you host the program again, but if you don't have the resources, this could motivate you to find a way to make the program happen again. In the event that a program, or service, does not have the best turnout, evaluate it anyways. You might discover a simple way to make the program more attractive to more participants, and there is no harm in trying to make a program work once you have the information and data you need to make it work. If you try again and still don't have any success, scrap it and try something different. Given the many programming possibilities, it is always good to try different things as long as they meet the needs of the community. In addition to patron evaluation feedback, ask partners and colleagues for their feedback. These people have a stake in the success of your initiative as some of them have been there since the beginning and may have actually taken part in building and marketing it. While patrons see and experience the final product, staff and partners are able to provide input in how to gain further support and improve the programs and resources.

Another unique perspective can be given by the presenters, if you have them. While they have been asked to present on a specific topic, they can usually tell you on whether the library is presenting mental health programs in the most effective way. For example, would teens learn more from an interactive workshop or would they prefer to simply talk about the issue? While you may be familiar with the types of programs that appeal to teens, input from experts can help you decide what format will have the biggest impact on attendees. Lastly, asking presenters what they think worked well about the program will help you pitch similar ideas to other presenters. (To see customizable evaluation feedback forms, refer to Appendix B.)

Patron Feedback

As you review your programs, be sure to include patron feedback in your formal evaluations so that you can submit these comments to your supervisors. You can keep them as notes for drafting your master plan. If you prefer to keep patron feedback separate from your own report, create a simple online survey with Survey Monkey or Google Forms, which can be handed out at an event or posted online.

What's great about online survey programs is they are free or available at low cost. If your library has a budget and is willing to pay for this type of program, the premium version of Survey Monkey is helpful, as you can create an unlimited number of questions, create a customized URL, and export data into a PDF or Excel spreadsheet. If not, you can use the free version without all the bells and whistles. If you prefer using Google's products, Google Forms are easy to make, so, whatever your preference is, these products will get the job done neatly and efficiently. Of course, you can also create paper forms and hand them out to participants before they leave the library.

Whichever format you use, keep your questions general, so you can use them for other programs besides mental health programs. To see what an evaluation form looks like, please refer to Appendix B. While patron program evaluations capture the results of the program, staff program evaluations provide an in-depth look into how the program was implemented, who was part of the process, and if patrons got something worthwhile out of the programs. By compiling all of this information, you can provide your stakeholders with an overview of the program's effectiveness. In your program evaluations, see if you can note what you can do to meet the expectations of attendees. A sample of this form that can be customized can also be found in Appendix B.

DEVELOP A MASTER PLAN

Another reason to document and evaluate the teen mental health initiative is that it will provide a framework and direction for the future. If the community responds favorably to the mental health programs and resources, and you wish to create an expanded initiative, the library will need a master plan. A master plan provides direction for the library, community, and partners involved. While it is easy to confuse master plans and strategic planning, it is important to recognize that these are actually different concepts. What exactly is the difference between the two? A master plan envisions the future and how it will accomplish its long-term goals. In other words, the library and its partners can develop a more in-depth and detailed plan for the teen mental health initiative.

The first step in developing this plan is for the library and its partners to define what the long-term goals for the initiative are and describe how they will develop strategies to accomplish those goals. Remember to focus on the planning process and the long-term goals, or future, of your teen mental health initiative rather than on the methods the library can initiate to achieve the long-term goals (which would be the "strategy"). If you are not familiar with master planning, here are some simple online articles that will give a more detailed overview of the master plan process:

"How to Do a Master Plan in Nine Easy Steps." Planning for Complete Communities in Delaware. https://www.completecommunitiesde. org/planning/landuse/nine-step-master-plan/.
Rademacher, Susan. "Developing Effective Master Plans." RSS. December 31, 2008. https://www.pps.org/article/masterplan1.

As you develop your master plan, recognize that this process is going to take time. Just like building your mental health initiative, consider prioritizing your goals by identifying what is a short-term goal versus a long-term goal. The last thing you want to do is to overwhelm yourself by thinking you have to have a plan ready to go in six months. In fact, give yourself plenty of time to accomplish the integral parts of the plan first, which includes developing and supporting partnerships, additional staff training, and working with the teen community.

PLANNING THE FUTURE WITH PARTNERS

Although it does take time, the master-planning process doesn't have to be complicated. Depending on the size, and goals, of your initiative, work with a core group of partners to develop your master plan. As you and your partners develop your teen mental health initiative, always remember to keep an open line of communication. By checking in with your partners, periodically, you are actively engaging them, which will help you sustain these relationships. When you begin the master-planning process, ask your partners if they have other partners who may be able to assist with the planning process. Once you have identified partners who are able to assist you, ask them to be a part of the master-planning committee, which will take the library's teen mental health initiative to the next level.

If you are not familiar with the process of forming a planning committee, the first step is to include partners who will gain the most from your teen mental health initiative. For example, if your public health department has been assisting you with your teen mental health programming, ask them to be a part of this committee. If NAMI or local mental health groups have volunteered their time to talk with your teens as well, invite them to join in the planning process as this master plan will help them spread their services to all parts of the community. Note that not all of your partners will have the time to dedicate to this process; always keep them in the loop, as they may be able to help in other capacities, such as providing networking contacts or marketing your initiative.

Once you have established your planning committee, ask your partners if they have developed a master plan of their own. If your partners have developed a similar plan, ask them to share their process. If not, start with the basics of master planning and let it evolve as you work together. There is a lot of flexibility with how to create a master plan. As long as the library and partners have a shared vision for the future, start strategizing on how to accomplish your goals as a committee. As you work with partners, keep your supervisor and upper management informed. By keeping your management up to date, they will be able to answer any question the committee may have in regard to policy and funding.

Since master plans focus on the future, it is important to think about how far into the future you wish to plan. Basically, this will be determined by your goals. With the success of your teen mental health programs and services in mind, work with your committee to see what a reasonable timeline would be to develop the long-term goals. Understand that mental health research and information is continually evolving. In other words, if you develop a ten-year plan, there is a chance you will have to adjust your plan along the way. Once the library and its partners have decided on the timeline, other elements will help in creating the long-term goals.

As you discuss long-terms goals, there are several things to consider in determining how these goals will be accomplished. First of all, develop criteria, or a set of questions, that will help you evaluate whether or not an objective can be feasibly implemented. Here are some questions/criteria that might help you evaluate your goals and objectives:

- How will these goals be funded? (i.e., will funding come from a specific budget or will additional funding, such as grants funding, be needed)
- How much time will staff and partners dedicate to accomplish these goals? (i.e., does the library have adequate staff to support this goal or can partners assist)
- Identify organizations that would be willing to commit their services to support these goals (i.e., identify organizations such as medical schools or nonprofits that can provide free and confidential services to teens)
- What kinds of marketing campaigns will be implemented to advertise these goals? (i.e., how will this service be advertised and who will assist in advertising efforts)

- How will the committee obtain feedback to continue supporting these goals? (i.e., how will the library quantify the number or services or resources used)

As you organize and prioritize the goals of the master plan, use the data gathered from the initiative to establish the objectives of the master plan. For example, if teens stated that they would attend onsite counseling services at the library, use your evaluation criteria to determine the following:

- What organization will provide the counseling services?
- Who will fund the counseling services?
- How will the library market this service?
- What kinds of policies and procedures have to be developed to protect teen privacy?
- Will the service require appointments or will it be a drop-in service?
- Will services be offered every day or once or twice a week?

This is just a sampling of questions to consider when evaluating your objectives. As you work with the committee, your criteria may evolve, which isn't necessarily a bad thing as long as the group is able to develop objectives that can be accomplished.

As mentioned previously, prioritize your objectives based on how quickly they can be completed and what may take a little longer. By setting realistic goals, the committee can draft a cohesive plan that will accomplish the goals of the master plan within the intended time frame. In other words, imagine a master plan as a road map where the destination is known, but the group will have to figure out how to get there in an efficient way. While there may be detours and a couple of u turns, always persist. If you have to take a little longer to get there, know that you will eventually arrive at your destination, which is the end goal.

For more information on program planning and evaluation, and building partnerships, check out the following resources:

"Engaging the Community More Fully in the Library—Creating Collaborative Partnerships in the Community." Florida Library Webinars. October 13, 2015. https://floridalibrarywebinars. org/engaging-the-community-more-fully-in-the-library-creating-collaborative-partnerships-in-the-community-ondemand/.

Goulding, Anne. "Engaging with Community Engagement: Public Libraries and Citizen Involvement." *New Library World* 110, no. 1/2 (January 9, 2009): 37–51. doi:10.1108/03074800910928577.

"Program Evaluation Forms." ACRL TechConnect. 2015. https://acrl. ala.org/IS/is-committees-2/resources-for-officers-and-committee-chairs/program-evaluation-forms/.

Public Library Association. "Planning & Evaluation." United for Libraries. July 30, 2018. http://www.ala.org/pla/resources/tools/directors-managers-administrators/planning-evaluation.

"Sample Survey." Infopeople. May 15, 2013. https://infopeople.org/sites/default/files/webinar/2013/05-15-2013/Sample_Survey.pdf.

"Santa Clara County Library District Program Evaluation." Santa Clara Library District. http://spot.sccl.org/forms/SCCLD_program_eval_form.pdf.

"Six Steps of Program Evaluation." Northwest Center for Public Health Practice. 2018. https://www.nwcphp.org/evaluation/tools-resources/program-evaluation-tips.

Starr, Rebecca. "Program Evaluations: Helpful Tool or Necessary Evil?" Programming Librarian. August 5, 2015. http://www.programminglibrarian.org/blog/program-evaluations-helpful-tool-or-necessary-evil.

8

◇ ◇ ◇

CREATING A SELF-CARE PLAN

Developing a teen mental health initiative is not an easy task. Not only does it take time; it takes a lot of energy, attention, and dedication as well. In addition to your daily tasks, you can expect the process will substantially add to your workload and create stress, which is why it is important to develop a self-care plan. This chapter guides you in making this plan.

When you think about self-care, consider the practices you already engage in to destress. Also, think about the things that cause you a lot of stress and how you actively manage that stress. If you have yet to develop a self-care plan, start planning one now. Why? Because by acknowledging your limits and finding ways to recover your balance, you will be more productive and more self-aware of your own mental health.. Implementing a teen mental health initiative should not cause unnecessary stress, so be open and honest to yourself and recognize that you have your limits. In fact, you need to make yourself a priority, because without you, the initiative may not develop the way it should.

THE IMPORTANCE OF SELF-CARE

According to Mental Health America, "Taking good care of yourself is paramount to the success of your recovery process. People in recovery find that their physical, spiritual, and emotional health are all connected, and that supporting one supports the others."[1] Now you may be thinking, "I'm not in recovery!" For a lot of people, recovery is synonymous with someone who is struggling with an illness. However, recovery can apply to anyone who experiences an event that has a profound effect on their well-being. In other words, recovery can apply to you when you experience a moment of extreme stress or even distress. By developing a self-care plan, you are creating a method to help regulate and rebalance your emotions. Whether it is dealing with a difficult patron or assisting a teen during a mental health crisis, this plan can help you process your emotions, regulate your mind and body, and help you to refocus. The goal of this self-care plan is to ensure that you are doing your utmost to care for your well-being. As a librarian, you are an important part of a team, where your dedication and energy have a profound effect on not just the library but the patrons as well. In order to serve teens with mental illness, you, yourself, need to have the fortitude to step in when needed, which is why you should have a self-care plan.

HOW TO DEVELOP A SELF-CARE PLAN

Lisa D. Butler states, "[t]here is no one-size-fits-all self-care plan, but there is a common thread to all self-care plans: making a commitment to attend to all the domains of your life, including your physical and psychological health, emotional and spiritual needs, and relationships."[2] You may already employ self-care plan, but now is a good time to review it. Creating, or expanding, a self-care doesn't have to be difficult. In fact, there is a methodology for creating a self-care plan that can be used to create a plan to meet your specific needs. Here are some recommendations from the University of Buffalo to consider when developing your plan.

Identify the stressors in your life

Think about the things that cause you stress, such as relationships, health issues, a long commute to work, and/or responsibilities to others such as family members or children. While these commitments may bring you joy, think about how they also take you away from doing other things you should be doing or want to do. If you have other interests and commitments, you probably find yourself pulled in a million directions that can be overwhelming or exhausting. While it is natural to have some stress in life, be mindful if you notice any changes in your body and your mood. Believe it or not, stress doesn't only affect your mind; it has an impact on your body, which is why it's important to pay attention to it while under duress. Also, note what situations or routines that cause the most stress. By taking inventory of your stressors, you will be able to identify what they are and employ self-mechanisms to help you manage your stress.

What self-care mechanisms you have in place now?

Given the stress, or stressors, in life, what tools do you use to help destress or unwind? Consider the activities, people, and objects that make you feel happy or help you relax. Also, when you use these tools, note how your body responds. For example, if you work out for 30 minutes, notice how you feel. If you feel better, physically or mentally, these activities are your self-care, or coping, mechanisms you can use to manage stress.

What habits or routines do you engage on a daily basis to support your well-being?

Think about the things you do, or participate in, that make you feel happy or good. These habits and routines can take on a variety forms, so focus on the ones that really have an impact on your mind and your body. Whether it's running a mile, painting a portrait, grabbing dinner with friends, or spending time with your furry loved ones, these activities provide you with relief, and hence it is something that you need to do. Through these outlets, you are giving yourself the opportunity to manage stress, which can help you develop coping skills when life is a little too difficult.

What coping mechanisms do you employ when you are in distress?

While it's a good idea to have a few coping mechanisms, think about developing a variety of skills to fit your environment. For example, what do you do to destress after dealing with a difficult patron? Do these activities actually make you feel better? In fact, do these mechanisms help you prevent stress when you know you're about to enter a stressful situation? If they do, these are the coping skills you will want to develop when you feel like you're going to fall apart.

In the event of an emergency, when you feel overwhelmed, what mechanisms do you have in place?

Whatever skills you decide to employ in each situation, again, pay attention to your body. If you become so frustrated that you notice your pulse is racing and your muscles are becoming tense, this is your body's reaction to stress. If you find yourself in this situation often, it's definitely a sign that you are becoming overwhelmed, which is why you need to employ any, or all, your coping skills to bring your mind and body back to center. If you find that your coping skills aren't working in a particular situation, it's okay to take yourself out of that situation, especially at work. If you need to step away from a discussion or need your coworker to take over, that's the best thing you can do for yourself. If you want to do your best, your mind and body need to be in sync, so don't feel ashamed if you have to just walk away.

Make a commitment to follow your self-care plan

Once you recognize your self-care mechanisms and how you will use them, create a plan and stick to it. Whether you write it down or memorize it, this plan should guide you through any situation. If you feel like you need to make adjustments, or add new mechanisms, do what you have to do to make sure that you care for yourself no matter how big or small the situation may be. Remember there is only one you, which is why it is necessary to develop a plan that is realistic and appealing to you. Lastly, this plan should be about you and only you, so don't feel like your coping mechanisms have to include, or impress, those close to you.

Be kind to yourself

Always, always be kind to yourself. While it's part of your job to be kind to others, apply that logic to yourself. Also remember, your teens like you for a reason, which is why you should like you for who you are simply because they like you. By showing kindness to yourself, you are giving yourself the care and the confidence you need to do your job, so always appreciate the qualities that make you a good librarian. Moreover, continue to be kind to yourself, especially when you make mistakes.

Learn to forgive yourself

If mistakes are made, learn to forgive yourself. As a teen librarian, you put your heart and soul into everything you do, and sometimes things just don't work out the way they should. In such times, allow yourself to reflect on what happened and learn from it. There is absolutely no use in beating yourself up over something that happened in the past, so focus on the future. Once you develop this habit, continue to learn and grow, but also be proud of what you have done as well.

Share your success with your trusted friends and family members

There is nothing wrong with sharing your triumphs with your friends and family. Whatever your support system may be, it's always a good thing to tell them of your accomplishments as it reaffirms to them you are doing just fine. By communicating with your support system, you are showing them that you are okay because they are the first ones to spot when you aren't feeling good. If you haven't been sharing good news in a while, chances are your support system may be worried about you. However, you can tell them you are actually doing okay, or better, by telling them that you have developed a plan that is helping you cope with life.

These recommendations are by no means exhaustive. In fact, there is a lot of information available to create your own self-care plan, but, keep in in mind, you don't have to include every single recommendation to create the right self-care plan. All self-care plans are based on individual's needs, so if you know certain things will work for you, and some won't, that is fine. In fact, if you search online for self-care plans, you'll find many worksheets that you can download and tailor to your needs. Whatever method you choose or whatever worksheet you fill out, the most important aspect of a self-care plan is to focus on you. If you already have a self-care plan that works for you, it won't hurt to see how you can improve what you are doing by integrating other practices to support your well-being. For more suggestions on how to build a self-care plan, check out the following resources:

Websites:

Butler, Lisa D. "Developing Your Self-Care Plan." *Developing Your Support System—University of Buffalo School of Social Work—University at Buffalo,* July 12, 2016. https://socialwork.buffalo.edu/resources/self-care-starter-kit/developing-your-self-care-plan.html.

"Developing a Self-Care Plan." *ReachOut Schools,* 2018, http://schools.au.reachout.com/articles/developing-a-self-care-plan.

Worksheets:

Jeffries, Carolyn, and Shari Tarver-Behring. "SUN Program: How to Create and Individualized Self-Care Plan." Department of Education Psychology & Counseling. California State University Northridge, March 2015. https://www.csun.edu/sites/default/files/SUN-Self-care-Plan.pdf.

TECHNIQUES TO PREVENT WORKPLACE BURNOUT

Once you find a self-care plan that works for you, think about how your plan can help you prevent burnout on the job. As a librarian, you not only work with the public, which can be demanding, you also work with colleagues who can be just as difficult. According to Mayo Clinic, "Job burnout is a special type of job stress—a state of physical, emotional or mental exhaustion combined with doubts about your competence and the value of your work."[3] Signs of job burnout can include the following:

- Inability to be productive at work
- Irritability with customers and colleagues
- Experiencing aches and pains such as headaches and/or body aches
- Having trouble sleeping or eating
- Always feeling tired or exhausted
- Feeling cynical or disillusioned with the job

If you are experiencing any, or all, of these feelings, you may develop workplace burnout, which can have an impact on how you function as a librarian. While a lot of people experience these feelings sometimes, developing a self-care plan can assist you in managing these feelings. However, if these feelings are constant or causing a significant impact on your ability to function in general, consider consulting a mental health professional as these could be anxiety-related signs. By recognizing a change in your behavior, you can manage these feelings using a self-care plan, which should contain strategies and techniques to help you process your emotions when you feel overwhelmed.

Creating Boundaries at Work

As you employ your self-care plan, consider how you can create boundaries. Whether it's at work or at home, creating healthy boundaries will help you not just manage your stress but create a habit that prevent further stress. What exactly does it mean to create boundaries? By creating boundaries, you are identifying what behaviors are acceptable and what are unacceptable to you. In addition to these behaviors, the boundaries you set help you determine what you can do to change things and what you can't do. If you are not sure whether you need to set boundaries, consider the following:

- Does a colleague, or patron, do something that really bothers or angers you?

- Is there something about your work environment that you wish you can change?
- Do certain tasks bother you more than others?
- Do you bring work home with you?

If you answered "yes" to any, or all of these, you will want to consider setting boundaries for these stressors as they could lead to workplace burnout.

Boundaries can take on all kinds of forms. The most visible boundaries are the ones that you express to others. For example, let's say you have a coworker who likes to ask a lot of personal questions. You can simply ignore his or her questions or change the subject. While this may work for some, it may be painful for others, which is why it's important to set boundaries by verbally informing a person that you are not comfortable with these types of questions. By speaking with this person directly, you are making it very clear what your boundaries are. Furthermore, this declaration puts the person on notice that you will not tolerate certain behaviors. If the person continues to cross those boundaries, there is no shame in removing yourself from the situation by speaking with a supervisor or asking another colleague for help.

This type of situation can also happen with patrons. As a teen librarian, you know that teens will tell you all kinds of things that you probably don't want to know. Whether it's about school, friends, or their family, teens might seek you out because they trust you. It may seem natural that teens will want to tell you personal things about themselves but understand that you are not their therapist. Does that mean you cannot be sympathetic to what they are feeling? Of course not. But depending on what teens are divulging, you have the right to tell teens that what they are telling you is inappropriate. Just like your nosy coworker, teens can push your limits, so make sure to create boundaries between you and your teens. As much as you want to help every teen you come across, there is only so much you can do. If you believe a teen is in need of mental health resources, do the best that you can to help the teen. As a librarian, your job is to help teens get the information they need to thrive and survive. If a teen continues to ask you for help to the point where you have exhausted all your resources, consider calling your mental partners for assistance. Whatever the case may be, know that you have done the best you can. It can be difficult to enforce boundaries with teens; understand that you are not doing this to be mean or unfeeling—you are doing this to preserve your own sanity and well-being. As a teen librarian, you are important part of your organization. Without your passion and dedication to teens, they would not have the resources and services they need to thrive, which is why you need to take care of yourself. By setting boundaries with colleagues, and teen patrons, you are maintaining the best version of yourself that the library needs on a daily basis.

Meditation Exercises

Along with creating boundaries, consider incorporating practices and routines that support your sense of well-being. Meditation is a technique you can easily incorporate into your daily routine. What is great about meditation is that it doesn't require any equipment and you don't have to pay an exorbitant amount of money to learn how to do it. If you already mediate, you definitely understand the benefits of this practice. However, if you are not familiar with mediations, it may be worth looking into, as it has been used in many capacities, such as lowering blood pressure to helping people with substance use disorders.

Meditation is a practice with Buddhist origins, where practitioners focus on transforming the mind to develop skills such as concentration and a sense of calm. The practice incorporates techniques such as sitting postures, clearing the mind of thought, deep breaths, and repeating mantras. The most important aspect of this practice is to find a quiet place to settle into. If you want to mediate at work, find a place where you will have little to no disruption. If you have an office, close the door and turn of the lights to ensure that you won't be disturbed. Once you establish a place to practice meditation, you have everything you need to relax and calm your mind. Here are some instructions to get started:

1. Sit or lie comfortably.
2. Close your eyes.
3. Breathe naturally (don't force your breath).
4. Focus on your breathing and your body moves with the breath. Notice how your chest, shoulders, and rib cages move, naturally.
5. If your mind wanders, return your focus back to your breath.
6. Maintain this meditation practice for two to three minutes to start, and then try it for longer periods.

For more information about meditation for beginners, log on to the following website:

https://www.gaiam.com/blogs/discover/meditation-101-techniques-benefits-and-a-beginner-s-how-to#disqus_thread.

Here are some additional recommendations if you are interested in learning more about meditation:

Books:

Chavan, Yesenia. *Meditation for Beginners: How to Relieve Stress, Anxiety and Depression and Return to a State of Inner Peace and Happiness.* Vancouver Island, B.C.: Evita Publishing, 2014.

Davich, Victor N. *8 Minute Meditation: Quiet Your Mind, Change Your Life.* New York: The Penguin Group, 2014.

Kornfield, Jack. *Meditation for Beginners.* Boulder, CO: Sounds True, 2008.

Reninger, Elizabeth. *Meditation Now: A Beginner's Guide: 10-Minute Meditations to Restore Calm and Joy, Anytime, Anywhere.* Berkeley, CA: Althea Press, 2014.

Websites:

Boyes, Alice. "5 Meditation Tips for Beginners." *Psychology Today.* Sussex Publishers, March 18, 2013. https://www.psychologytoday.com/us/blog/in-practice/201303/5-meditation-tips-beginners.

Koreyva, Wendy. "Learn to Meditate in 6 Easy Steps." *The Chopra Center*, March 9, 2018. https://chopra.com/articles/learn-to-meditate-in-6-easy-steps.

Physical Exercise

Once you understand the basics of meditation, note how your body responds to taking a few moments to sit quietly and breathe. Since meditation has the ability to transform the mind, it can have positive effects on the body as well. In other words, it's good to pay attention to how your body responds to stress as well. Mediation exercises can certainly help you manage stress levels, but consider incorporating simple physical exercises that can help manage stress. According to the Centers for Disease Control and Prevention (CDC), "[t]here are numerous health benefits related to physical activity. These health benefits include a lower risk of chronic diseases such as diabetes, heart disease and stroke, some cancers, and depression."[4]

It can be difficult to squeeze in exercise while juggling desk time, meetings, and programs. However, it is not impossible, and you can even incorporate routines while at work. For example, during your lunch break, take a walk around your building to get your heart rate up. Also, if you have access to stairs and are able to climb stairs, consider taking the stairs to get where you need to. If you spend the majority of your time sitting, get up from your desk every now and then and stretch your muscles. Depending on your library budget, see if you can get a desk that raises and lowers to alter your position from sitting to standing as you work. If that is not an option, set an alarm to alert you to stand at least every 30 minutes. The whole point of exercise is to get your blood pumping and, in combination with meditation, bring oxygen to the brain so you can have more energy to function throughout the day.

Along with exercise, be sure to take regularly scheduled breaks. As a dedicated teen librarian, you may be tempted to not take breaks as your mind and body are going a million miles an hour. However, by the end of the day, observe how you feel. Do you feel even more tired? Does your body ache? This occurs because you haven't taken the time to stop and care for yourself. Often times, these bad habits can lead to serious health conditions that can affect your ability to work. While it's great to be excited and energetic, always take time to care your mind and body. If you don't move as much during your shift, be sure to take time either before or after work as physical activity helps the body unwind and relax.

To learn more about how you can stretch and exercise at work, check out these resources:

Books:

Swanson, Larry, and Joan Vernikos. *Scared Sitless: The Office Fitness Book*. Seattle: Elless Media, LLC, 2014.

Vranich, Belisa. *Breathe: The Simple, Revolutionary 14-Day Program to Improve Your Mental and Physical Health*. New York: St. Martin's Griffin, 2016.

Videos:

Mishler, Adriene, director. *Yoga at Your Desk. Yoga at Your Desk*, YouTube. November 5, 2014.www.youtube.com/watch?v=tAUf7aajBWE.

"Office Exercises You Can Do at Work." Performance by Bob Schrupp, and Brad Heineck, YouTube. September 27, 2016. www.youtube.com/watch?v=GIUwLNAxesA.

Websites:

Smith, Jacquelyn. "The 10 Best Exercises to Do at Your Desk." *Forbes*, Forbes Magazine. August 16, 2016. www.forbes.com/sites/jacquelynsmith/2013/02/06/the-10-best-exercises-to-do-at-your-desk/.

"A Workout at Work: 12 Office Exercises." *The Washington Post*, WP Company. September 26 2011. www.washingtonpost.com/graphics/health/workout-at-work/?noredirect=on.

Daily Affirmation

When you think about daily affirmations, what comes to mind? Does it seem like a silly practice? Do you think it helps? Do you live by certain affirmation or know of any that helps you cope with life? Daily affirmations actually do have a positive effect on your well-being. Looking at the definition of "affirmation," affirmation comes from the verb "to affirm," which is to declare a statement or proposition to be true. Based on this definition, daily affirmations are statements about an idea that a person believes to be true, which is why he or she practices them on a daily basis. Carmen Harra (2017) states that "[a]ffirmations do indeed strengthen us by helping us believe in the potential of an action we desire to manifest. When we verbally affirm our dreams and ambitions, we are instantly empowered with a deep sense of reassurance that our wishful words will become reality."[5] Here are some affirmations that Harra recommends as life changing:

"I am the architect of my life; I build its foundation and choose its contents."

"I have been given endless talents which I begin to utilize today."

"I possess the qualities needed to be extremely successful."

"My ability to conquer my challenges is limitless; my potential to succeed is infinite."

"Many people look up to me and recognize my worth; I am admired."

"I am a powerhouse; I am indestructible."

While there are endless types of affirmations and many books of ready-made affirmations are available, the ones that matter the most are the ones that mean the most to you. In other words, the affirmations that you apply to your daily lives are tools to help you cope and transform into the person you want to be. Consider writing a set of personalized affirmations for yourself. As you create a list of daily affirmations, look for statements that inspire you to be the best you can be. This practice should focus on words that you identify with and want to apply to your life. Affirmations should also encourage you when you feel down or anxious. Why? Affirmations should include practical approaches that will help you overcome your struggles while reaffirming that you are capable of achieving your goals.

Working with teens with mental illness will have a significant impact on your well-being. Memorizing, and repeating to yourself, words of encouragement can help calm your mind. In fact, by repeating these affirmations to yourself, you are actually training your brain to believe that you are able to achieve your goals. In this case, these words of encouragement, in conjunction with other techniques outlined in your self-care plan, provide a shell to protect or comfort you in times of need. Again, this may seem silly, but it is a great way to rebalance during stressful times and focus on the success the future will bring.

By caring for your mind and body, you are able to be the best version of yourself. By managing stress through self-care, you can help yourself foresee and overcomes obstacles that can affect your ability to function. Library school doesn't offer courses in self-care, so it's important to educate yourself and create that self-care plan that you have been meaning to do since last year. While "self-care" has become a buzz word lately, really look at the core of what it means: to care for yourself and do what you need to make sure you are protected and nurtured. Just like the saying states, "an apple a day . . . keeps doctor away," caring for your mind and body, mentally and physically, is just as important as nutrition to give yourself the breaks it needs to renew your mind, body, and spirit.

NOTES

1. "Taking Good Care of Yourself." *Mental Health America*. November 18, 2013. http://www.mentalhealthamerica.net/taking-good-care-yourself.
2. Butler, Lisa D. "Developing Your Self-Care Plan." Developing Your Support System—University at Buffalo School of Social Work—University at Buffalo. July 12, 2016. https://socialwork.buffalo.edu/resources/self-care-starter-kit/developing-your-self-care-plan.html.
3. Mayo Clinic Staff. "Know the Signs of Job Burnout." *Mayo Clinic*, Mayo Foundation for Medical Education and Research. September 17, 2015, www.mayoclinic.org/healthy-lifestyle/adult-health/in-depth/burnout/art-20046642.
4. "Physical Activity." *Centers for Disease Control and Prevention*, Centers for Disease Control and Prevention. September 28, 2017. www.cdc.gov/physicalactivity/worksite-pa/index.htm.
5. Harra, Carmen. "35 Affirmations That Will Change Your Life." *The Huffington Post*, TheHuffingtonPost.com. June 15, 2017. www.huffingtonpost.com/dr-carmen-harra/affirmations_b_3527028.html.

Appendix A

Resources for Teens, Parents, and Teen Advocates

TEEN MENTAL HEALTH FICTION SUGGESTIONS

Abuse/Assault

Anderson, Laurie Halse. *Speak*. New York: Square Fish, 2011.
Christopher, Lucy. *Stolen*. Frome, UK: Chicken House, 2013.
Hartzler, Aaron. *What We Saw*. New York: HarperTeen, 2015.
King, A. S. *Reality Boy*. New York: Little, Brown & Company, 2014.
Kuehn, Stephanie. *Complicit*. New York: St. Martin's Griffin, 2016.
McGinnis, Mindy. *The Female of the Species*. New York: Katherine Tegen Books, 2017.
Mesrobian, Carrie. *Sex & Violence*. Minneapolis: Carolrhoda Lab, 2015.
O'Neill, Louise. *Asking for It*. New York: Quercus, 2016.
Perry, Jolene B. *Stronger Than You Know*. Chicago: Albert Whitman & Company, 2014.
Werlin, Nancy. *The Rules of Survival*. New York: Speak, 2011.
Wolf, Jennifer Shaw. *Breaking Beautiful*. New York: Walker Books, 2014.
Zarr, Sara, and Kyra Sedgwick. *Story of a Girl: A Novel*. New York: Little, Brown & Company, 2017.

Addiction

Burgess, Melvin. *Smack*. New York: Square Fish, 2010.

Desir, Christa. *Other Broken Things*. New York: Simon Pulse, 2017.

Hopkins, Ellen. *Crank*. New York: Margaret K. McElderry Books, 2013.

Horowitz, Lena. *Dancing with Molly: A Novel*. New York: Simon Pulse, 2016.

Kern, Peggy. *Little Peach*. New York: Balzer + Bray, 2015.

Nelson, Blake. *Recovery Road*. New York: Scholastic, 2015.

Reed, Amy Lynn. *Clean*. New York: Simon Pulse, 2012.

Saenz, Benjamin Alire. *Last Night I Sang to the Monster*. El Paso, TX: Cinco Punto Press, 2012.

Woodson, Jacqueline. *Beneath a Meth Moon: An Elegy*. New York: Penguin Group USA, 2013.

Anxiety Disorders

Federle, Tim. *The Great American Whatever*. New York: Simon & Schuster BFYR, 2017.

Kinsella, Sophie. *Finding Audrey*. New York: Random House Children's Publishers, 2015.

Lockhart, E. *The Boyfriend List (15 Guys, 11 Shrink Appointments, 4 Ceramic Frogs and Me, Ruby Oliver)*. New South Wales: Allen & Unwin, 2016.

Martinez, Jessica. *Virtuosity*. New York: Simon Pulse, 2012.

Miller, Lauren. *All Things New*. Los Angeles: Three Saints Press, 2017.

Ness, Patrick. *The Rest of Us Just Live Here*. New York: HarperTeen, 2016.

Reichardt, Marisa. *Underwater*. New York: Square Fish, 2017.

Whaley, John Corey. *Highly Illogical Behavior*. New York: Speak, 2016.

Attention-Deficit Disorder (ADD)/Attention-Deficit Hyperactivity Disorder (ADHD)

Costa, T. L. *Playing Tyler*. Nottingham, UK: Angry Robot, 2013.

Page, Katherine Hall. *Club Meds*. New York: Simon Pulse, 2006.

Priemaza, Anna. *Kat and Meg Conquer the World*. New York: HarperTeen, 2017.

Roe, Robin. *A List of Cages*. Westport, CT: Hyperion, 2017.

Autism Spectrum Disorder

Choldenko, Gennifer. *Al Capone Does My Shirts*. New York: Puffin Books, 2014.

Erskine, Kathryn. *Mockingbird*. New York: Philomel Books, 2010.

Haddon, Mark. *The Curious Incident of the Dog in the Night-time*. New York: Vintage Contemporaries, 2011.

Kelly, Tara. *Harmonic Feedback*. New York: Henry Holt, 2010.

Stork, Francisco X. *Marcelo in the Real World*. New York: Scholastic, 2011.

Bipolar Disorder and Depression

Colbert, Brandy. *Little & Lion*. New York: Little, Brown & Company, 2018.

Kletter, Kerry. *The First Time She Drowned*. New York: Speak, 2017.

Levithan, David. *Every You, Every Me*. New York: Random House Publishing Group, 2012.

Lord, Emery. *When We Collided*. London: Bloomsbury, 2017.

Niven, Jennifer. *All the Bright Places*. New York: Random House Children's Books, 2016.

Reed, Amy Lynn. *Crazy*. New York: Simon Pulse, 2013.

Sones, Sonya. *Stop Pretending: What Happened When My Big Sister Went Crazy*. New York: HarperTeen, 2016.

Vizzini, Ned. *It's Kind of a Funny Story*. Westport, CT: Hyperion Paperbacks for Children, 2007.

Eating Disorders

Anderson, Laurie Halse. *Wintergirls*. New York: Viking, 2009.

Colbert, Brandy. *Pointe*. New York: G.P. Putnam Sons, 2014.

Friend, Natasha. *Perfect*. Minneapolis: Milkweed Editions, 2004.

Haston, Meg. *Paperweight*. New York: HarperTeen, 2017.

Lange, Erin Jade. *Butter*: New York: Bloomsbury, 2012.

Reed, Amy Lynn. *Clean*. New York: Simon Pulse, 2012.

Shahan, Sherry. *Skin and Bones*. Park Ridge, IL: Albert Whitman & Company, 2015.

Impulse Control/Self-Harm

Desir, Christa. *Bleed Like Me*. New York: Simon Pulse, 2015.

Hassan, Michael. *Crash and Burn*. New York: Balzer + Bray, 2014.

McCormick, Patricia. *Cut*. New York: Push, 2011.

Moskowitz, Hannah. *The Break*. New York: Simon Pulse, 2009.

Obsessive-Compulsive Disorder (OCD)

Green, John. *Turtles All the Way Down*. New York: Penguin, 2018.

Haydu, Corey Ann. *OCD Love Story*. New York: Simon Pulse, 2014.

Ness, Patrick. *The Rest of Us Just Live Here*. New York: Harper Collins, 2015.

Stone, Tamara Ireland. *Every Last Word*. Los Angeles: Hyperion, 2017.

Toten, Teresa. *The Unlikely Hero of Room 13B*. New York: Ember, 2018.

Vaughn, Lauren Roedy. *OCD, the Dude, and Me: A Novel*. New York: Dial Books, 2013.

Wilson, Rachel. *Don't Touch*. New York: HarperTeen, 2014.

Post-Traumatic Stress Disorder (PTSD)

Anderson, Laurie Halse. *The Impossible Knife of Memory*. New York: Speak, 2015.

Doller, Trish. *Something Like Normal*. New York: Bloomsbury, 2013.

Murdoch, Emily. *If You Find Me*. New York: St. Martin's Griffin, 2014.

Quick, Matthew. *Boy 21*. New York: Little, Brown, 2013.

Skilton, Sarah. *Bruised*. New York: Amulet Books, 2014.

Woolston, Blythe. *Freak Observer*. Minneapolis: Carolrhoda Books, 2012.

Schizophrenia

Leavitt, Martine. *Calvin*. New York: Square Fish, 2017.

Schindler, Holly. *A Blue so Dark*. Woodbury, NY: Flux, 2010.

Sheff, Nic. *Schizo*. New York: Speak, 2015.

Shusterman, Neal, and Brendan Shusterman. *Challenger Deep*. New York: HarperTeen, 2016.

Trueman, Terry, and Mechthild Hesse. *Inside Out*. Stuttgart, Germany: Klett Sprachen, 2012.

Wolitzer, Meg. *Belzhar*. New York: Speak, 2015.

Suicide

Ford, Michael Thomas. *Suicide Notes: A Novel*. New York: HarperTeen, 2010.

Forman, Gayle. *I Was Here*. New York: Speak, 2016.

Hand, Cynthia. *The Last Time We Say Goodbye*. Sydney, New South Wales: HarperCollins, 2015.

Quick, Matthew. *Forgive Me, Leonard Peacock*. London: Headline, 2014.

Warga, Jasmine. *My Heart and Other Black Holes*. New York: Balzer + Bray, 2016.

Book-to-Movie

It's Kind of a Funny Story. Directed by Anna Boden and Ryan Fleck. Performed by Zack Galifinakis and Keir Gilchrist. Universal City: Universal, 2010. Film.

Miss Peregrine's Home for Peculiar Children. Directed by Tim Burton. Performed by Eva Green, Rupert Everett, Samuel L. Jackson, and Asa Butterfield. Century City: Twentieth Century Fox, 2016. Film.

The Perks of Being a Wallflower. Directed by Stephen Chbosky. By Stephen Chbosky. Produced by Lianne Halfon, Russell Smith, and John Malkovich. Performed by Logan Lerman, Emma Watson, and Ezra Miller. United States: Lionsgate, 2012. Film.

TEEN MENTAL HEALTH NONFICTION BOOKS

Bakewell, Lisa. *Mental Health Information for Teens: Health Tips about Mental Wellness and Mental Illness, Including Facts about Recognizing and Treating Mood, Anxiety, Personality, Psychotic, Behavioral, Impulse Control, and Addiction Disorders*. Detroit: Omnigraphics, 2014.

Bornstein, Kate. *Hello Cruel World*. New York: Random House, 2006.

Breel, Kevin. *Boy Meets Depression, or, Life Sucks and Then You Die/or, Life Sucks and Then You Live*. New York: Harmony Books, 2015.

Carlson, Dale, Michael Bower, and Carol Nicklaus. *Out of Order: Young Adult Manual of Mental Illness and Recovery: Mental Illnesses, Personality Disorders, Learning Problems, Intellectual Disabilities & Treatment and Recovery*. Branford, CT: Bick Publishing House, 2013.

Dunkle, Elena, and Clare B. Dunkle. *Elena Vanishing: A Memoir*. San Francisco: Chronicle Books, 2016.

Edelfield, Bruce, and Tracey J. Moosa. *Drug Abuse*. New York: Rosen Publishing, 2012.

Hollander, Barbara Gottfried. *Conduct Disorder.* New York: Rosen Publishing, 2014.

Jamieson, Patrick E., and Moira A. Rynn. *Mind Race: A Firsthand Account of One Teenager's Experience with Bipolar Disorder.* New York: Oxford University Press, 2006.

Letran, Jacqui. *I Would, but My Damn Mind Won't Let Me!: A Teen's Guide to Controlling Their Thoughts and Feelings.* Asheville, NC: Healed Mind, 2016.

Lezine, DeQuincy A., and David A. Brent. *Eight Stories Up: An Adolescent Chooses Hope over Suicide.* Oxford: Oxford University Press, 2008.

Palmer, Libbi. *The PTSD Workbook for Teens: Simple, Effective Skills for Healing Trauma.* Oakland, CA: New Harbinger, 2013.

Porterfield, Jason. *Teen Stress and Anxiety.* New York: Rosen Publishing, 2014.

Roza, Greg. *Cutting and Self-injury.* New York: Rosen Publishing, 2014.

Schab, Lisa M. *Beyond the Blues: A Workbook to Help Teens Overcome Depression.* Oakland, CA: Instant Help Books, 2008.

Schab, Lisa M. *The Anxiety Workbook for Teens: Activities to Help You Deal with Anxiety & Worry.* Oakland, CA: Instant Help Books, 2008.

Shannon, Jennifer, and Doug Shannon. *The Anxiety Survival Guide for Teens: CBT Skills to Overcome Fear, Worry & Panic.* Oakland, CA: Instant Help Books an Imprint of New Harbinger Publications, 2015.

Shapiro, Lawrence E. *Stopping the Pain: A Workbook for Teens Who Cut and Self-injure.* Oakland, CA: New Harbinger Publications, 2008.

Snyder, Kurt, Raquel E. Gurd, and Linda Wasmer Andrews. *Me, Myself, and Them: A Firsthand Account of One Teenager's Experience with Schizophrenia.* New York: Oxford University Press, 2007.

Toner, Jacqueline B., and Claire A. B. Freeland. *Depression: A Teen's Guide to Survive and Thrive.* Washington, DC: Magination Press, American Psychological Association, 2016.

MENTAL HEALTH BOOKS FOR PARENTS, CAREGIVERS, AND MENTORS

Evans, Dwight L. *If Your Adolescent Has Depression or Bipolar Disorder: An Essential Resource for Parents.* New York: Oxford University Press, 2006.

Jensen, Frances E., and Amy Ellis Nutt. *The Teenage Brain: A Neuroscientist's Survival Guide to Raising Adolescents and Young Adults.* New York: Harper, 2015.

Mondimore, Francis Mark, and Patrick Kelly. *Adolescent Depression: A Guide for Parents.* Baltimore: Johns Hopkins University Press, 2015.

Riera, Michael. *Uncommon Sense for Parents with Teenagers.* Berkeley, CA: Celestial Arts, 2004.

Shatkin, Jess P. *Child & Adolescent Mental Health—A Practical, All-in-One Guide.* New York: W.W. Norton & Company, 2015.

Siegel, Daniel J. *Brainstorm: The Power and Purpose of the Teenage Brain.* New York: Penguin Group USA, 2014.

Walsh, B. Timothy, and V. L. Cameron. *If Your Adolescent Has an Eating Disorder: An Essential Resource for Parents.* New York: Oxford University Press, 2006.

White, Aaron M., and Scott Swartzwelder. *What Are They Thinking?!: The Straight Facts about the Risk-Taking, Social-Networking, Still-Developing Teen Brain.* New York: W.W. Norton & Company, 2013.

RESOURCES FOR TEENS ON MENTAL ILLNESS

Medline Plus-Teen Mental Health

Website: https://medlineplus.gov/teenmentalhealth.html

National Alliance on Mental Illness (NAMI)—Teen and Young Adults

Website: https://www.nami.org/Find-Support/Teens-and-
Young-Adults

National Institute on Mental Health—Childhood and Adolescent Mental Health

Website: https://www.nimh.nih.gov/health/topics/child-and-
adolescent-mental-health/index.shtml

Society for Adolescent Health and Medicine—Resources

Website: https://www.adolescenthealth.org/Resources/Clinical-
Care-Resources/Mental-Health/Mental-Health-Resources-For-
Adolesc.aspx

Teen Line

Website: https://teenlineonline.org/
Physical Address:
Teen Line
Cedars-Sinai
P.O. Box 48750 Los Angeles, CA 90048–0750
Phone:
(310) 855-HOPE (4673)
(800) TLC-TEEN (852–8336) (U.S. & Canada only)

TeenMentalHealth.org

Website: http://teenmentalhealth.org/
Physical Address: 5850 University Ave. PO Box 9700. Halifax, Nova
Scotia, Canada, B3K 6R8
Phone: 1 + (902) 470–6598

Appendix B

Resources for Teen Librarians

NATIONAL RESOURCES ON MENTAL DISORDERS

National Alliance on Mental Illness
Website: https://www.nami.org/
Find a local chapter: https://www.nami.org/About-NAMI
Address: 3803 N. Fairfax Drive, Suite 100 Arlington, VA 22203
Main phone: 703-524-7600

National Institute on Mental Health
Website: https://www.nimh.nih.gov/
Address: 6001 Executive Boulevard, Rockville, MD 20852
Main phone: 1-866-615-6464

Substance Abuse and Mental Health Services Administration
Website: https://www.samhsa.gov/
Address: 500 Fishers Lane, Rockville, MD 20857
Main phone: 877-726-4727

TRAINING RESOURCES ON MENTAL DISORDERS

California State Library Mental Health Initiative

Webinars
Teen Mental Illness 101
https://infopeople.org/civicrm/event/info?id=629&reset=1

Teen Suicide Prevention: How to Listen, Assess, and Guide Teens in Their Time
of Need
https://infopeople.org/civicrm/event/info?id=668&reset=1

Becoming Trauma-Informed and Resiliency-Focused and Informed
https://infopeople.org/civicrm/event/info?id=706&reset=1

How to Use the Community Resiliency Model to Assist Teens in Need
https://infopeople.org/civicrm/event/info?id=715&reset=1

Training videos
California Library Services
https://www.youtube.com/channel/UCnSA9yKFJNxKLTzG49aiSVw

Youth Mental Health First-Aid Certification Information

Mental Health First Aid USA
Website: https://www.mentalhealthfirstaid.org/
E-mail: MHFAinfo@thenationalcouncil.org
Phone: 1-888-244-8980, ext. 4
Hours: Monday–Friday 8:30 AM–5:00 PM ET

TEEN MENTAL HEALTH INITIATIVE

Patron Program Evaluation

Did this program help you find the information you need?   Yes   No

Did this program make you want to learn more about this topic?   Yes   No

If so, do you plan on checking out materials on this topic?   Yes   No   Maybe

How would you rate this program on a scale of 1 to 5

1   2   3   4   5

Would you recommend this program to your friends or family?   Yes   No

Would you like to attend a similar program?   Yes   No

How did you hear about this program?

❏ Library website   ❏ Newsletter   ☒ Facebook   ❏ Ad   ❏ Health Care Provider

☒ School   ❏ Friend   ❏ City website   ❏ Other

Suggestions for future programs?

_____

_____

_____

_____

_____

_____

Comments:

_____

_____

_____

_____

_____

_____

TEEN MENTAL HEALTH INITIATIVE

Program Evaluation

Department: _____   Staff Contact: _____

Name of Event: _____

Brief Description: _____

_____

_____

_____

Presenter Name: _____

Presenter Organization: _____

Presenter Contact Information: _____

                                               Address: _____

                                               E-Mail: _____

                                               Phone: _____

Patron Feedback:

_____

_____

_____

Performer/Presenter Feedback:

_____

_____

_____

Staff Notes:

_____

Repeat Program?   Yes _____   No _____

SELF-CARE RESOURCES

Chavan, Yesenia. *Meditation for Beginners: How to Relieve Stress, Anxiety and Depression and Return to a State of Inner Peace and Happiness*. Vancouver Island, BC: Evita Publishing, 2014.

Davich, Victor N. *8 Minute Meditation: Quiet Your Mind, Change Your Life*. New York: The Penguin Group, 2014.

Kornfield, Jack. *Meditation for Beginners*. Boulder, CO: Sounds True, 2008.

Reninger, Elizabeth. *Meditation Now: A Beginner's Guide: 10-Minute Meditations to Restore Calm and Joy, Anytime, Anywhere*. Berkeley, CA: Althea Press, 2014.

Swanson, Larry, and Joan Vernikos. *Scared Sitless: The Office Fitness Book*. Seattle, WA: Elless Media, LLC, 2014.

Vranich, Belisa. *Breathe: The Simple, Revolutionary 14-Day Program to Improve Your Mental and Physical Health*. Seattle, WA: St. Martin's Griffin, 2016.

Websites

Boyes, Alice. "5 Meditation Tips for Beginners." *Psychology Today*. Sussex Publishers, March 18, 2013. https://www.psychologytoday.com/us/blog/in-practice/201303/5-meditation-tips-beginners.

Inner IDEA. "Meditation 101: Techniques, Benefits, and a Beginner's How-To." *Gaiam*, March 9, 2018. www.gaiam.com/blogs/discover/meditation-101-techniques-benefits-and-a-beginner-s-how-to.

Koreyva, Wendy. "Learn to Meditate in 6 Easy Steps." The Chopra Center. March 9, 2018. https://chopra.com/articles/learn-to-meditate-in-6-easy-steps.

Smith, Jacquelyn. "The 10 Best Exercises to Do at Your Desk." *Forbes*, Forbes Magazine. August 16, 2016. www.forbes.com/sites/jacquelynsmith/2013/02/06/the-10-best-exercises-to-do-at-your-desk/.

"A Workout at Work: 12 Office Exercises." *The Washington Post*, WP Company. September 26, 2011. www.washingtonpost.com/graphics/health/workout-at-work/?noredirect=on.

Videos

Mishler, Adriene, director. *Yoga at Your Desk*. *Yoga at Your Desk*, YouTube. November 5, 2014. www.youtube.com/watch?v=tAUf7aajBWE.

"Office Exercises You Can Do at Work." Performance by Bob Schrupp and Brad Heineck, *Office Exercises You Can Do at Work*, YouTube. September 27, 2016. www.youtube.com/watch?v=GIUwLNAxesA.

INDEX

ABOUT THE AUTHOR

DEBORAH K. TAKAHASHI is a branch librarian for Pasadena Public Library who specializes in Youth Services. She holds an MLS degree and is certified in Youth Mental Health First Aid. She is a 2009 ALA Spectrum and 2010 CLA Edna Yelland scholar. She served as the 2015–2017 Social Media Co-Chair for the California Library Association (CLA) Youth Services Interest Group and was a member of the Mental Health Advisory Committee for the 2016–2017 California State Library (CSL) Mental Health Initiative. She writes for ALA's Young Adult Library Services Association (YALSA) blog.